FEAR
and other names of the
ENEMY

FEAR
and other names of the
ENEMY

DONNA M. YOUNG

FEAR and Other Names of the Enemy
Copyright © 2019 by Donna M. Young. All rights reserved.

No part of this publication may be reproduced, stored in a retrieval system or transmitted in any way by any means, electronic, mechanical, photocopy, recording or otherwise without the prior permission of the author except as provided by USA copyright law.

Unless otherwise indicated, all Scripture quotations are from *The Holy Bible, English Standard Version*®, copyright © 2001 by Crossway Bibles, a publishing ministry of Good News Publishers. Used by permission. All rights reserved.

Published by Donna M. Young
P O Box 76, Lawton, IA 51030
dmywriting@wiatel.net

Author photo by Elizabeth Rose Kahl

Book Cover and Layout by Christina Hicks
christinahickscreative@gmail.com

Published in the United States of America
soft cover: 978-1-947143-14-2
E-Book: 978-1-947143-15-9
Non-Fiction / General
Non-Fiction / Christian General

http://www.donnamyoungwriting.com

TABLE OF CONTENTS

Foreword 7
Satan's Many Names—FEAR. 13
Satan's Many Names—Regret. 33
Satan's Many Names—Doubt/Unbelief . . 51
Satan's Many Names—Guilt and Shame . 69
Satan's Many Names—Hate 89
Satan's Many Names—Envy and Jealousy 107
Satan's Many Names—Pride and Arrogance 127
Satan's Many Names—Grief and Despair 143
Satan's Many Names—Helplessness
    and Hopelessness 157
Satan's Many Names—Anxiety and Stress 173
Satan's Many Names—Self Righteousness 187
Satan's Many Names—Un-forgiveness . . 209
Opening Our Eyes 225
Who is Our Infinite God? 245
Who Does the World Say We Are? 277

Conformed to the Image of His Son.... 301
How Shall They Hear? 317
Good is Evil and Evil is Good-Losing
    Sight of the Holy Truth 333
The Truth About Your Enemy......... 353
The Good News 363
Helps.............................. 369
Fruits of the Spirit.................. 371

FOREWORD

Some have asked me why I chose to focus on the topic of FEAR for this book. My answer: because no matter who you are; what faith, or lack thereof, drives you; no matter your profession, or life's experiences; we have all been afraid at one time or another. We have all experienced that stabbing pain in the pit of our stomach; the bewilderment and confusion of not knowing; the terror, as it goose steps down your spine; or the overwhelming sense that you might be the one and only person in the universe too dreadful to love.

Some of us thought we were pretty tough, coming up. Or, at least we tried to make everyone around us think we were. But, FEAR was always creeping around in the back of our mind messing with our thoughts and creating panic. FEAR causes us to feel stressed, beyond our ability to cope. FEAR causes us to make poor choices and bad decisions. And, FEAR decimates families and relationships.

FEAR makes us believe we are worthless and unworthy; shameful and not sufficient; deserted and alone; not attractive enough; or worst of all, not loved, even by the one who is the epitome of LOVE. Remember, FEAR is one of the many names of the enemy, and just like all facets and names of the enemy, FEAR is a liar.

I struggled with FEAR for many decades in my life, and almost allowed myself to be completely choked out by its stranglehold on my heart and mind, but Jesus...... Don't you love that? But Jesus. The most beautiful proclamation of enduring and powerful truth we know, is that unquenchable, undeserved, unconditional love of God. I even love the pause we take when we exclaim, "But Jesus".

Jesus has taught me through His boundless Grace and Love that His Truth is more commanding, more healing, more real and more sure than ANY name of the enemy.

Through experiences in my personal cancer journey, and through the survival of abuses in my childhood, I finally came to realize that; even when I felt completely alone and forgotten; Jesus was right beside me, and had been all along.

We all have a story to tell. I have discovered that it is in the sharing of our stories with one another, that we feel most connected and less afraid of what the future might bring. Through this desire to be personally linked together, pre-programmed into our humanity by God, we can create a way to lift one another out of the depths of despair, and into the light of the Lord's love. Jesus is the answer. He is the only way to blessed peace in our hearts and minds throughout this journey we call life. Only by the Grace and Love of our Lord can we overcome FEAR and ALL the Names of the Enemy.

The Lord is my light and my salvation; whom shall I fear? The Lord is the stronghold of my life; of whom shall I be afraid?

Psalm 27:1

SATAN'S MANY NAMES —FEAR

One might wonder what I mean by, "Many Names"?

Its pretty simple, really. Just as Jesus has many names: 'Savior', 'Redeemer', 'Lord', 'Prince of Peace', 'Healer of the Nations', 'Lamb of God', among others; so does our enemy. He is first, and foremost, Satan. But his other names are significant as well. 'The Evil One', 'The devil', 'The tempter', 'The god of this world', 'The great dragon', and 'The old serpent', just to name a few.

I am not a big fan of giving Satan more attention than he deserves. But, it seems the world has taken to either pretending he doesn't exist, or making light of him. You know, the guy in bright, red spandex, sporting horns and a pitchfork? How about all those great Halloween costumes and Sunday morning cartoon strips? The ridiculous caricatures abound, so much so, that even small children no longer fear him, much less take him seriously. That, my friends, can be a very costly mistake. And though we shouldn't obsess about him, we do need to clear up misconceptions about his purpose. Yes my friends, Satan has a purpose. A very real and very evil one.

We must learn to recognize him, in all his names and forms, in order to call him out and confront him in the Name of Jesus. And though, as Christians, we certainly want to focus our minds most on Christ and those things closest to His heart. It is also important to note that Our Lord spent time talking about the nature of this very real enemy and warning us not to fall for his deception. So, I believe it is appropriate for us to prepare ourselves for his attacks and to do what Jesus has clearly told us to do.

Having correct facts about the devil is admittedly not a salvation issue. But we need to have good information, for this reason: if we are sharing our faith with someone who has wrong beliefs about the devil, then, it stands to reason that individual probably has misconceptions about Hell. And if that individual doesn't clearly understand Hell, then he, or she, will most likely not see their need for a Savior to forgive their sins and keep them out of that place. Ultimately, getting our information and facts in line about our adversary can be a real life saver.

In researching information for this book I discovered something that surprised me. This is that the notion of there not actually being a real devil is a fairly new lie. Modern theology is the main culprit here. All through the centuries people knew there was a devil and they greatly feared him. Hence, they desired a relationship with the Lord, for reasons of self preservation if nothing else. Though that isn't the optimal reason for an ongoing relationship with the Savior, it is a start that can be built upon.

Liberal theologians have so watered down the facts about Satan and his minions that they have caused more recent generations to believe perhaps the devil isn't even real. They are convinced the idea of an evil being, like the devil, is most likely based on fables from a primitive society. And that certainly we don't need to fear those silly superstitions. Or, I've even heard, perhaps the concept of demons is simply a personification of the evil that is within us all.

So, why are modern theologians doing this? Why are they telling us lies that are opposite of what the Bible assures us is true? They are saying it because, sadly, and to their own and many other's detriment, they have come to believe their own lies. Due to that, Satan is now using them mightily to perpetuate those falsehoods, prompting them to promote these untruths so we will lower our guard. We cannot allow that to happen. So, what proofs can we read in the Word? What does the Bible say? Let's see for ourselves.

Does God think there is a real devil?

"Now there was a day when the sons (angels) of God came to present themselves before the Lord, and Satan also came among them. The Lord said to Satan, "From where have you come?" Satan answered the Lord and said, "From going to and fro on the earth, and from walking up and down on it." Job1:6-7

How about Jesus? Does He believe in Satan? I believe His view on the subject is pretty clear from these and other scriptures.

"And He said to them, "I saw Satan fall like lightning from heaven." Luke 10:18

"I will no longer talk much with you, for the ruler of this world (Satan) is coming. He has no claim on me, but I do as the Father has commanded me, so that the world may know that I love the

Father. Rise, let us go from here. John 14:30

Let's see how Paul felt about this issue. Is there a real devil?

"Anyone whom you forgive, I also forgive. Indeed, what I have forgiven, if I have forgiven anything, has been for your sake in the presence of Christ, so that we would not be outwitted by Satan; for we are not ignorant of his designs." 2 Corinthians 2:10,11

How about Peter? Did he believe there was a real Satan?

"Be sober-minded; be watchful. Your adversary the devil prowls around like a roaring lion, seeking someone to devour." 1 Peter 5:8

However, even though we can see quite clearly from scripture that Satan is real; the average person walking around on the streets and even many, so called, Christians simply don't believe there is a devil. Many, who have not read, or studied, the Word, believe that perhaps the church has made him up, and perpetuated a myth, in order to keep us in line. To scare us into submission if you will. Now, why would Jesus have spent time speaking about Satan if he was not real? God, after all, is not a man that He should lie.

I believe some people are afraid to admit there might be a Satan, because then they would have to admit there is a hell. If there is a hell and they don't trust Jesus as Savior and Lord, they would necessarily be going there. Therefore, if we don't acknowledge Satan, we don't have to admit there is a hell and our future is more hopeful? Perhaps in someone else's mind that makes sense, but I have learned in my life that ignoring something does not make it go away. I'm here to tell you that there is no hope aside from Jesus, so that particular way of thinking is not productive at all and will have a most terrible ending.

Many people; some of the same people who go about seeking a supernatural solution in other names and places, while simultaneously, refusing to lean on Jesus; tap into unspeakable powers they do not understand. Playing with Ouija boards, or figuring their horoscopes to predict their futures. Some delve into Wiccan rituals, using the powers of 'Mother Earth' to cast spells; some join covens; or contact fortune tellers and witch doctors to solve their problems. These powers are very scary and very real indeed. Most of the people who are indiscriminately using them, have been fooled as to where the powers originate. Since they don't believe the source of that power, Satan, actually exists, they are unaware of how very dangerous this is.

Yes beloved, evil (Satan) is a person. Just as Grace and Truth (Jesus) is a person. And, Jesus took that person seriously. He called him the god of this world in *2 Corinthians 4:4 "In their case the god of this world has blinded the minds of the unbelievers, to keep them from seeing the light of the Gospel of the glory of Christ, who is the image of God."*

If you are not 'Born Again', Satan will do everything in his power to keep you that way. If you are a child of God, he hates you, just as he hates God, the Bible and anything that contains the Truth of the glorious Gospel of Jesus Christ. I am convinced his two least favorite books of the Bible are Genesis and Revelation. Genesis, because we see him for who he really is, when he deceives the woman God created with lies that ripple through the thousands of generations to follow. Revelation, because it tells of his well deserved demise in the lake of fire. Though he is a terrifying foe, you, as a child of the Most High God, don't need to fear him, not if you have trusted Jesus for eternal life. Because, if you are born again, your debt has been paid, and you will reign victorious with the Savior for eternity; over Satan, the defeated foe.

Satan loves the fact that many no longer believe he exists. It makes his nefarious job infinitely easier. I found a song, written and performed by a Christian singer, song writer, Keith Green, in the 1970s. Look him up online. He has many great Christian offerings. The song is entitled "No One Believes in Me Anymore", and subtitled, "The Devil's Boast." Though it was written more than four decades ago, read the lyrics and see if it doesn't ring some pretty frightening bells even now.

Well, my job keeps getting easier as time keeps slipping away.

I can imitate the brightest light, and make your night look just like day.

I put some truth in every lie to tickle itching ears.

I'm drawing people just like flies, 'cause they like what they hear.

I'm gaining power by the hour, they're falling by the score.

It's getting very simple now, since no one believes in me anymore.

"Heaven's just a state of mind," my books read on your shelf.

Have you heard that God is dead? I made that one up myself!

They're dabbling in magic spells, they get their fortunes read.

They heard the truth, but turned away and followed me instead.

I used to have to sneak around, but now they just open their doors.

No one's watching for my tricks, since no one believes in me anymore.

Everyone likes a winner - with my help, you're guaranteed to win.

Hey, man, you're not a sinner - no, you've got the truth within.

And as your life slips by, you'll believe the lie

that you did it on your own.

But I'll be there to help you share a dark eternal home.

My job keeps getting easier as day slips into day.

The magazines, the newspapers print every word I say.

This world is just my spinning top, it's all like child's play.

I dream that it will never stop, but I know it's not that way.

Still my work goes on and on, always stronger than before.

I'm going to make it dark before the dawn, since no one believes in me anymore.

Remember that when you were saved, you were brought into a battle that has been raging since before time as we know it. Not a safe and sweet Sunday school picnic, or a religious playground; but a toe-to-toe, put up your dukes, no-holds-barred, knock down drag out fight against the most menacing enemy of all time. We are literally up against the demonized, mobilized forces of hell.

Jesus, the one who loves us unconditionally, unflinchingly, and so sacrificially that He was willing to die for us, was aware of the power of the devil. So much so, that He taught us to pray, this way, in Matthew 6:9-13:

> *"Our Father in heaven,*
> *hallowed be Your name.*
> *Your kingdom come,*
> *Your will be done,*
> *on earth as it is in heaven.*

Give us this day our daily bread,
and forgive us our debts,
as we also have forgiven our debtors.
And lead us not into temptation,
but deliver us from evil: For Yours is the kingdom,
and the power, and the glory, forever. Amen"

The prayer He taught us included, "But, deliver us from evil", which may rightly be translated, "Deliver us from the Evil One." And, why do we need deliverance? Because Satan is potent. The devil is a supernatural individual with unholy, dark, supernatural powers. He is not to be trifled with, especially if you are not personally secure in your salvation.

But, we must also remember that He followed, "But deliver us from the Evil One." With, "For Yours is the kingdom, and the power, and the glory, forever. Amen." Reminding us that the devil might be powerful, but God is ALL - powerful.

The kingdom does not ultimately belong to that old serpent, Satan. It belongs to the Lord, Jesus Christ.

"And the Lord will be king over all the earth. On that day the Lord will be one, and His Name one." Zechariah 14:9

And those who follow Satan are going to end up exactly where Satan ends up, for Hell is, "Prepared for the devil and his angels."

FEAR is crippling and debilitating, but Hope is stronger than fear. Hope is essential. It is the vehicle that faith stands on. God calls us to be brave, when we confront the evil one. Remember that bravery is not the absence of FEAR, but the pushing ahead, and marching forward, in spite of it. Call on the Name of Jesus, and the enemy must flee.

A friend once said to me, "You have every God given right to be afraid. After all the things you went through as a kid. The abuse and suffering. And everything your first two husbands put you through. I wouldn't blame you if you spent the rest of your life scared to death." I thought about that for some time. And I realized, I was allowing FEAR to scare me literally to death. FEAR was making me sick; it was stressing me out; it was causing me to jump at every sound; it was making me leery of friendships and relationships; and it was causing me to mistrust everyone in my path, including those God had placed there. FEAR isn't a God given right! It is a tool, a face, a lie of the enemy. Once I finally began to see it as such, my life changed dramatically for the better.

Always remember: *"There is no fear in love, but perfect love casts out fear. For fear has to do with punishment, and whosoever fears has not been perfected in love." 1 John 4:18*

I am continually encouraged by the many scripture verses where God reminds us not to FEAR. Not because of 'who' we are, but 'whose' we are.

"But now thus says the Lord, He who created you, O Jacob, He who formed you, O Israel: Fear not, for I have redeemed you; I have called you by name, you are mine." Isaiah 43:1

I have fought the good fight, I have finished the race, I have kept the faith,

2 Timothy 4:7

SATAN'S MANY NAMES —REGRET

My main intent in writing this book, was to help ordinary people avoid this one. Oh, I don't mean just any old regret, though it might be nice to be rid of it all. I'm referring to the biggest regret of all.

What does the Bible say about regret? The Bible refers to regret as a way for Satan to get inside of your mental state, (or inside your head, if you will). Regret can be devastating if we don't keep it in check. According to notes left behind for loved ones, in the wake of tragedy, it is the biggest reason for acts of suicide. I urge you to live with no regrets. But look forward, for your reward is coming.

I know I look forward to mine. We have been promised that there will be nothing to compare with that day. However, for those who have not yet repented of their sins; which means they have never turned away from those sins and forsaken them, trusting in Jesus for their salvation; there is only a fearful expectation of the coming wrath of God that will lead to the ultimate regret for time without end.

"Then I saw a great white throne and Him who was seated on it. From His presence earth and sky fled away, and no place was found for them. And I saw the dead, great and small, standing before the throne, and books were opened. Then another book was opened, which is the book of life. And

the dead were judged by what was written in the books, according to what they had done. And the sea gave up the dead who were in it, Death and Hades gave up the dead who were in them, and they were judged, each one of them, according to what they had done. Then Death and Hades were thrown into the lake of fire. This is the second death, the lake of fire. And if anyone's name was not found written in the book of life, he was thrown into the lake of fire." Revelation 20:11-15

What a regret, huh? The definition of Regret is: Sadness, repentance, or disappointment over something that has happened or been done. Especially a lost or missed opportunity.

One might wonder how anyone could come to end up in the lake of fire? I mean, I thought God was a merciful God. Isn't He? I thought He was a God of love. Why would He condemn anyone to hell if He cares so much?

Hello dear ones. As a friendly reminder, His Word is filled with one warning after another about hell. We actually hold the book, which has all the details from beginning to end for mankind, in our hands. This book (the Bible) gives us a blow by blow account of the creation, rise, downfall, and second chance for God's creation, if we so choose to accept that second chance. The choice is ours and ours alone. And it is literally a choice between Heaven and Hell.

I have actually been asked this question. "So, I thought we didn't have to 'work' for our salvation? Is God a liar?" Oh come on now people. So, accepting a free gift is work? I'm not sure that even the laziest human being on the planet could perceive that accepting a free gift from God is work.

"For by Grace you have been saved through faith. And this is not your own doing; it is the gift of God, not a result of works, so that no one may boast." Ephesians 2:8,9

"God is not man, that He should lie, or a son of man, that He should change His mind. Has He said, and will He not do it? Or has He spoken, and will He not fulfill it?" Numbers 23:19

No we don't work for our salvation, and no, God does not lie. But Satan wants you to believe that God is a liar. He wants you to believe that God's Word cannot be believed. That salvation is difficult, is dependent on your goodness and can be easily lost. He wants you to believe you are too terrible to be saved, too horrible to love, or that

God has given up on you. Do not believe him.

Yes, regret is a sad thing. Yet even God had regrets. When, in Noah's age, He looked out and saw that mankind had become so evil that He couldn't find a single reason to keep them alive, He was very sad indeed.

"The Lord saw that the wickedness of man was great in the earth, and that every intention of the thoughts of his heart was only evil continually. And the Lord was sorry that He had made man on the earth, and it grieved Him to His heart. So the Lord said, "I will blot out man whom I have created from the face of the land, man and animals and creeping things and birds of the heavens, for I am sorry I have made them. But Noah found favor in the eyes of the Lord." Genesis 6:5-8

I never, ever, want to be one of God's regrets. I've

always tended to go my own way. And have been, in more ways than one, a walking contradiction. As a kid I was defiant, but painfully shy. As a young adult I was terrified, but faking my way through with a false bravado that only I knew was made up for the benefit of others. As a woman I was frightened beyond belief about almost everything; yet commanding and in charge, in work and life situations where I needed to take control. I never, for one single moment, felt 'good enough'. And my stomach was always a mess, shaking and nauseated. But for many years after I married Marty, and became the pastor's wife, I tried everything I could think of to make myself look holy in the eyes of others. I'm sure I was one of God's biggest disappointments during that time, yet somehow He continued to love me through it all.

Frank Sinatra sang a song entitled, 'My Way'. I'm a Sinatra fan, but I've never liked this particular song. It's morbid, sad, fatalistic, humanistic, defiant and openly arrogant. It's about a dying man, looking back over his life, feeling good about the fact that he did everything his way. Look at how entirely self centered the lyrics are. I wonder how many of us have lived our lives this way, never considering the part God might play in our lives? I know I did for more years than I ever liked to admit. Why is it so easy for human beings to fall in to this trap? Well, again, Satan.

The lyrics follow.

'My Way'

And now, the end is near,

FEAR and other names of the ENEMY

And so I face the final curtain.

My friend, I'll say it clear,

I'll state my case, of which I'm certain.

I've lived a life that's full,

I've traveled each and every highway.

And more, much more than this,

I did it my way.

Regrets, I've had a few,

But then again, too few to mention.

I did what I had to do,

And saw it through without exemption.

I planned each charted course,

Each careful step along the byway.

And more, much more than this,

I did it my way.

Yes, there were times, I'm sure you knew,

When I bit off more than I could chew.

> But through it all, when there was doubt,
>
> I ate it up and spit it out.
>
> I faced it all and I stood tall,
>
> And did it my way.
>
> I've loved, I've laughed and cried
>
> I've had my fill, my share of losing
>
> And now,…

There's something about this song that evidently releases an unhealthy, self-assertive energy in bars and karaoke restaurants in the Philippines. I read an unusual article which told about how people get into fights and literally start killing others while this song is playing. "My Way" has now been stricken from many nightclubs there because it fuels so many deadly fights. No one knows how many people have been killed during the singing of "My Way," but police in the Philippines have a subcategory of crime dubbed "My Way Killings."

I will note here that the "My Way" philosophy is the very essence of anti-Christian thinking. As believers, our aim is to please Christ in every way. We don't come to the point of death and look back over our lives with fatalistic defiance. We want to be able to say, "I have finished the work You gave me to do."

Our attitude should be: "I did it His Way."

And, regrets, I think I've had more than a few. I definitely tried to do it my way for a very long time. The problem with doing it my way, was that it usually wasn't the way God wanted me to do things. You know what is the strangest part? The things I regret most would likely surprise people.

I actually don't regret the mistakes I made,

like sneaking out of a second story window with my sister, and getting caught sneaking back in. Or the dumb things I've done, like trying my hand at drinking, smoking and shoplifting, but not being particularly successful at any of them. I just wasn't cool like that I guess. And how about this huge one; trying to abort my son. I was a scared, sixteen year old, rape victim after all. So, I can confidently say I didn't know anything. I do praise God that it didn't work, and that he is alive and well, eight children and three grand children later.

Those things, along with a million other dumb, arrogant, thoughtless and stupid things were opportunities for me to learn more about myself and the depths of depravity to which I was willing to stoop before finally surrendering my life to have a personal relationship with my Jesus. I also don't regret the illnesses I've gone through, or hardships that plague us all to one degree or another. I've finally discovered that it was in those hard, frightening, scary, terrifying and embarrassing moments that the Lord dealt with me, taught me, comforted me, and proved to me that He had never really left my side at all.

The regrets I do have? Those would be the times, looking back now, where I know God specifically placed someone in my path. Someone I was supposed to share Jesus with; someone I was supposed to comfort, or minister to in some way. These instances, of course, were before I believed in a Savior who loves me unconditionally. With my whole heart I wish I could go back and have a redo on those times, but alas, the opportunity has passed.

Yes, the times when I was too afraid, or embarrassed, to speak up and share the Gospel. Those are my regrets. I hope that each of the people who were placed before me, those that I did not witness to, were later placed in the path of a disciple with more faith than I had during that time. I guess I will never know. Yes, regrets, I've absolutely had more than a few.

I can only imagine the regret Peter felt, can't you? Do you remember this conversation?

"Peter answered Him, "Though they all fall away because of You, I will never fall away." Jesus said to him, "Truly, I tell you, this very night, before the rooster crows, you will deny me three times." Peter said to Him, "Even if I must die with You, I will not deny You." Matthew 26:33-35

I believe most of us know how that incident played out. If you don't know, or can't remember, continue reading in Matthew and you will discover that Peter did indeed deny Christ three times before the rooster crowed in the morning. What a devastating experience that must have been, to be forewarned as he was, and yet to still make a horrible decision like that anyway; to deny Christ.

But, hey, who are we to judge? With access to Bibles available in every arena of our lives, even down to apps on our smart phones. And with scripture to guide us in every possible scenario of our fast paced and complicated lives, don't we have all the same thoughtful forewarning necessary to make the right choices? I wonder how many, like Peter, like me, like you perhaps, ignore the Word for a period of time and take our own crooked and unproductive path?

Here's what I know now. These days, when God places a person in my path, I am no longer afraid, shy or embarrassed to disclose what is on my heart. I jump in with both feet, to share the Grace that I have been given with anyone who will listen. Now I know, from personal experience, what a miracle working, prayer answering, mighty healer God we serve. And I can't imagine not wanting to share this God, my God, with every person in the world who is placed before me.

"For godly grief produces a repentance that leads to salvation without regret, whereas worldly grief produces death." 2 Corinthians 7:10

I have discovered, just as Paul declared, that

we can't change the past. Regrets be damned. All we can do is pull ourselves up, lean upon Jesus, and move on. So, from now on, that is exactly what I will be doing. Praise God for second chances, and third, and fourth...........

"Brothers, I do not consider that I have made it on my own. But one thing I do: "forgetting what lies behind and straining forward to what lies ahead. I press on toward the goal for the prize of the upward call of God in Christ Jesus." Philippians 3:13,14

If any of you lacks wisdom, let him ask God, who gives generously to all without reproach, and it will be given him. But let him ask in faith, with no doubting, for the one who doubts is like a wave of the sea that is driven and tossed by the wind. For that person must not suppose that he will receive anything from the Lord, he is a double-minded man, unstable in all his ways.

James 1:5-8

SATAN'S MANY NAMES —DOUBT/UNBELIEF

Just as Jesus is the author and finisher of our faith, Satan is the author of Doubt. *Hebrews 12:2 (NKJV) looking unto Jesus, the author and finisher of our faith, who for the joy that was set before Him endured the cross, despising the shame, and has sat down at the right hand of the throne of God.* That scripture is a very good reason why the Lord is adamant about us not succumbing to doubt. However, God also knows His children, and He loves us anyway. Even when we mess up!

As in all things pertaining to the devil, doubt keeps us from experiencing the fullness of Christ's Love and the blessings thereof. It is difficult to receive blessings from a God who you sincerely believe is not capable, or willing, to bless you.

As a young woman I was filled with doubt. I had serious trust issues, and a very patchy and wavering faith, due to events that had taken place in my youth. Many years of sexual, physical, emotional and verbal abuse, by my biological father; followed later by physical, emotional and verbal abuse by my mom, and then my step-dad, led me to believe that if there really was a God, He certainly didn't care about me.

I doubted His desire to protect me. I doubted His ability to protect me. I even doubted my worthiness to be protected. I fretted all the time, leading to stomach problems, ulcers, nervous problems and constant headaches.

God knows it is easy to doubt. He's experienced that doubt from His children over and over again through the annals of time, as we can see in His Holy Word:

Remember Thomas? *"Now Thomas, one of the twelve, called the Twin, was not with them when Jesus came. So the other disciples told him, "We have seen the Lord". But he said to them, "Unless I see in His hands the mark of the nails, and place my finger into the mark of the nails, and place my hand into His side, I will never believe." Eight days later, His disciples were inside again, and Thomas was with them. Although the doors were locked, Jesus came and stood among them and said, "Peace be with you." Then He said to Thomas, "Put your finger here, and see my hands; and put out your hand, and place it in my side. Do not disbelieve, but believe." Thomas answered Him, "My Lord and my God!" Jesus said to him, "Have you believed because you have seen me? Blessed are those who have not seen and yet have believed." John 20:24-29*

Its important to note here that Jesus did not stop loving Thomas because he doubted; but He did make it a point to tell Thomas that those who believe without seeing will be blessed. Do we believe? Do we take the time to pursue God's best for us, or His purpose for our lives, by praying and delving into scripture? With the Word of God literally at our fingertips, in this modern, technological world, we can no longer say we have no way of seeing, and no way of knowing those things the Lord would have us know. God's Word makes Jesus just as real as if He is standing right before us.

A member of one of our congregations, a few years ago, said, "I'm not a big fan of reading scripture. Whenever I read the Bible, I feel like I'm responsible for all that new information. That scares me, because the more I know, the more likely I am to mess up." I told her then, and I will say so again, that the more we get to know the Lord, the more He will fill our hearts with the desire, and the way, to do the right thing. The Word of God inhabits our hearts and gives us the ability to know Him more intimately, and follow Him with more confidence. Don't ever let the FEAR of responsibility limit your desire to grow closer to your Father.

How about Sarah? Did she believe

unwaveringly? *"They said to him, "Where is Sarah your wife?" And he said, "She is in the tent." The Lord said, "I will surely return to you about this time next year, and Sarah your wife shall have a son. And Sarah was listening at the tent door behind him. Now Abraham and Sarah were old, advanced in years. The way of women had ceased to be with Sarah. So Sarah laughed to herself, saying, "After I am worn out, and my lord is old, shall I have pleasure?" The Lord said to Abraham, "Why did Sarah laugh and say, "Shall I indeed bear a child, now that I am old? Is anything too hard for the Lord? At the appointed time I will return to you, about this time next year, and Sarah shall have a son." But Sarah denied it, saying, "I did not laugh," for she was afraid. He said, "No, but you did laugh."*
Genesis 18:9-15

I'd like to point out that Sarah's doubt and unbelief did not cause the Lord to renege on His promises to Abraham, to make him the father of many nations. Even though the couple tried to force the promise of children through Sarah's handmaid Hagar; with the birth of Ishmael; God was still good to His Word and Isaac was ultimately born to fulfill the covenant. God is always good, even when we are not. Faith is a very powerful thing. And, Abraham's faith was accounted to him as righteousness.

Zechariah is another example of doubt in God's ability to follow through. When he and Elizabeth desired a child, he doubted what the angel Gabriel came to tell him. *"And Zechariah said to the angel, "How shall I know this? For I am an old man, and my wife is advanced in years." And the angel answered him, "I am Gabriel. I stand in the presence of God, and I was sent to speak to you and to bring you this good news. And behold, you will be silent and unable to speak until the day that these things take place, because you did not believe my words, which will be fulfilled in their time." Luke 1:18-20*

I find it quite interesting, that, though we always seem to pay some kind of price for our doubt, God continues to be faithful to fulfill His promises. I believe the Master's heart aches whenever we doubt His ability and especially His willingness to help us; just as our own hearts would ache if our children doubted us. It saddens me to think of times He has likely sat shaking His head, with heart aching in His chest, over my own episodes of doubt and fear. Elizabeth did indeed conceive and bear a son, John the Baptist, who would go before Jesus urging the world to repent. And, Zechariah did get his voice back.

And then, how can we ever forget, Moses. Moses doubted many things. Especially his own physical ability to do what the Lord was asking him to do. And, he continued to doubt, and question the Lord, until he caused God to be angry with him.

"But Moses said to the Lord, "Oh, my Lord, I am not eloquent, either in the past or since you have spoken to Your servant, but I am slow of speech and of tongue." Then the Lord said, "Who has made man's mouth? Who makes him mute, or deaf, or seeing, or blind? Is it not I, the Lord? Now therefore go, and I will be with your mouth and teach you what you should speak. But he said, "Oh, my Lord, please send someone else." Then the anger of the

Lord was kindled against Moses and He said, "Is there not Aaron, your brother, the Levite? I know that he can speak well. Behold, he is coming out to meet you, and when he sees you, he will be glad in his heart. You shall speak to him and put the words in his mouth, and I will be with your mouth and with his mouth and will teach you both what to do." Exodus 4:10-16

I will mention here (and not lightly) that God didn't strike Moses down for making Him angry. He also didn't 'get another guy'. He continued to use Moses, even though the man was obviously far from perfect. And, in spite of the fact that he continued to make mistakes. I'm personally very happy about that. Because, I'm just about as far from perfect as a human being can get, and yet, I know He uses me for His purpose.

He continually places people in my path who need to know the Lord. Because, He knows I am so filled with joy at the miracles He has done in my life, I can't help but share Him with everyone I meet. I don't think I could have made it this far in life, or trusted that I could be of any earthly use to the kingdom; with my writing, or anything else of worth; if I hadn't discovered the marvelous fact that He loves me in spite of my fallible humanity. And, I wouldn't have known that I was redeemable if there weren't so many accounts of regular, messed up people just like me, accomplishing remarkable things through Him.

The Bible is chock full of instances of God using ordinary people; to do extraordinary and remarkable things. Remember that the Father does not call the equipped, He equips the called, and we are all called to His purpose. I love knowing that I don't need to be perfect to be used. Doubt is no longer a prevailing theme in my life. I have been at the receiving end of enough blessings, to know for certain God loves me. I wish I could tell you that it didn't take those miracles and blessings for me to trust Him, but alas, I too was a doubting Thomas. I praise God that He is a Father of mercy and loves me anyway. So, encourage others. Show them how faith conquers all, even for those who have doubted.

"But you, beloved, building yourselves up in your most holy faith and praying in the Holy Spirit, keep yourselves in the love of God, waiting for the mercy of our Lord Jesus Christ that leads to eternal life. And have mercy on those who doubt, save others by snatching them out of the fire; to others show mercy

with fear, hating even the garment stained by the flesh." Jude 1:20-23

Some might wonder why I put Doubt and Unbelief in the same chapter. I did so because, though they are two completely different things; therefore two different names of Satan; I have often heard them used interchangeably. Due to that, I felt the need to address them together.

Doubt is simply a lapse in faith, whether it be a short lapse, or a long one; where unbelief is a well thought out process. When we doubt God's intent, willingness, or ability to help us, it is normally due more to our own sense of worthlessness. Unbelief is actually a completely different animal. Unbelief is the total turning away from the very existence of God, in any of His Triune forms, Father, Son, or Spirit. Have you ever heard that the only unforgivable sin is blaspheming of the Holy Spirit; or, in other words, refusing to admit the existence of, or authority within, of the power of God to transform? I should think this would be pretty obvious. If you have turned away, and you do not believe in the existence of the Father, the Son, or the Holy Spirit, how could you be saved by praying to the Father, about the sacrifice of His Son for you, to have the Holy Spirit come live inside you? Or, put even more simply. The only unforgiveable sin, is not allowing God to forgive you through the blood and sacrifice of His Son, Jesus Christ.

And, if you are wondering if you have committed the unpardonable, or unforgiveable sin? If indeed you are even contemplating whether or not you are doomed to hell? Then my answer to you, if you are still alive to read these words, is no. If you are still here, alive, and able to make a decision for Christ, then you can still do that. Problem solved! But, I urge you, please examine your heart and make that decision today. We never know what the next moment brings, much less the next day, week, or year. Make the most important decision, you will ever make, quickly, before Satan and his minions do something to take that decision from you.

"For God so loved the world, that He gave His only Son, that whosoever believes in Him should not perish but have eternal life. For God did not send His Son into the world to condemn the world, but in order that the world might be saved through Him. Whoever believes in Him is not condemned, but whoever does not believe is condemned already,

because he has not believed in the Name of the only Son of God. And this is the judgment: the light has come into the world, and people loved the darkness rather than the light because their works were evil. For everyone who does wicked things hates the light and does not come to the light, lest his works should be exposed. But whoever does what is true comes to the light, so that it may be clearly seen that his works have been carried out in God." John 3:16-21

"Whoever believes and is baptized will be saved, but whoever does not believe will be condemned. And these signs will accompany those who believe; in my Name they will cast out demons; they will speak in new tongues; they will pick up serpents with their hands; and if they drink any deadly poison, it will not hurt them; they will lay their hands on the sick, and they will recover." Mark 16:16-18

He does not deal with us according to our sins, nor repay us according to our iniquities. For as high as the heavens are above the earth, so great is his steadfast love toward those who fear Him; as far as the east is from the west, so far does He remove our transgressions from us.

                                      Psalm 103:10

SATAN'S MANY NAMES —GUILT AND SHAME

I thought I would deal with these two names of Satan together, because their causes and consequences are so similar. Satan loves to use Guilt and Shame against us, because if he can convince us that we have fallen too far to love; too far for God's forgiveness to reach; too far from redemption to be saved, he wins.

Growing up I know I felt terribly dirty and ashamed. Not just for stupid things I had done (and, believe me, I had done plenty), but for so many things that had been done to me. How could God love me, when my own parents acted as if they didn't care? How could He love me, if I couldn't even love myself?

Sexual sin is an especially touchy subject for many people. And, when we deal with sexual molestation of a small child, especially by a parent, we find that guilt and shame abound. At four years old, the first time my biological father raped me; I was not just physically injured, but wounded deep within my soul. This particular abuse continued for five and a half years. Terrified day and night, I developed stomach problems and headaches. I was terribly stressed and developed a nervous, jumpy demeanor that I dealt with for many years. I went to my mother for help. But, when I told her what he was doing to me, she slapped me so hard I was knocked solidly into the closet door. And I walked around with a red, swollen cheek for days. Leaving me with all the proof I needed, to know that I couldn't count on her or anyone else, each time I looked in the mirror.

That reaction from her caused me to never again have the courage to ask for help. She'd declined to believe what I was telling her then; refusing even to confront him; and she continued to look the other way for five and a half years. I felt deeply unworthy and broken beyond repair. Her growing alcoholism kept her in her own little world most of the time; beginning when I was very little and continuing for most of her life. So, giving her the benefit of the doubt, either she didn't see his actions, or simply refused to recognize the things he was doing to me, no matter how much damage was being done.

To my own detriment, I slowly became more defiant to the man who was abusing me, which earned me many additional beatings. I didn't care. Better that than the alternative. I vowed that he would never see me cry. Yet, at the very same time, I was dying inside. So vulnerable that I was painfully shy to the rest of the world. Feeling as if I wasn't good enough to look any 'normal' person in the eyes. And constantly trying to think of ways to get away from him, or to kill myself.

It wasn't until shortly before he turned himself into the police, when I was almost ten years old, that she was finally forced to acknowledge what was going on. We had moved to another city, since authorities were already searching for him on other charges, and our beds consisted of blankets on the floor of our new place. She walked into the room where I slept, saw him on top of me, and went to the kitchen to retrieve a cast iron skillet.

When she came back, she hit him so hard in the back of the head that I was fairly certain she'd killed him. I crawled out from under his limp form, sobbing. She stood for a few moments, shaking, tears streaming down her cheeks, before she turned and left the room. We never spoke of that moment again. He wasn't dead. But by then the police who had been on his trail for some time were getting close, so we packed up our few belongings and in a terrifying series of events, which blur together in their horror (and that I may speak of another time), made our way to the Canadian border.

I learned to deal with; or, to be honest,

ignore; my pain by turning within. I had what I considered to be a lightning bolt moment, early on. Reasoning that I couldn't rely on anyone, or trust anyone, including God. After all, hadn't I begged Him for help for years, only to be left very much alone in my suffering. I figured if He was real, He must be ignoring me, or worse, just didn't care enough to get involved.

After my biological father was sent to prison (for totally unrelated crimes), I thought I was finally free. But I discovered instead that my mother's drinking had grown to such a frightening extent, that she was perhaps even more physically and emotionally dangerous to me than he had been. Mom was devastated to have lost her 'soul mate'. Crushed by what she'd seen from the moment she'd walked into the room to witness his actions. But in her drunkenness, the reality had gotten a little mucked up in her head; and she somehow transferred, at least to some extent, the blame for his demise to me. I was the cause of it all.

She became horribly abusive; physically, emotionally and verbally. I can't tell you how many slaps, kicks and beatings I received at her hand. Or, how many times I went to school trying to cover the bruises on my back and arms. And this is to say nothing about the physical and sexual abuse I suffered at the hands of 'boyfriends' she brought home in the midst of her drunken 'loneliness'. But, much worse than the physical abuse, were the terrible things she said over and over to me.

Telling me she wished I'd never been born; that

she'd never wanted me, because I was supposed to be a boy, he'd wanted a boy after all and that's where all the trouble started; that I'd be better off dead; that I was ugly; that no one would ever love me; and on, and on. There were actually times, as I got older that I reasoned, in my own messed up mind, that perhaps she wasn't saying these things to hurt me. That maybe, just because they were indeed fact, and she was drunk after all, she needed to say them or she might explode.

I was filled with a guilt and shame I can't describe. And, as much as I am also ashamed to admit it, I even tried once to commit suicide by swallowing a whole bottle of sleeping pills. It didn't work, because someone found me. Like everything else in my life, failure after failure, I was unsuccessful at that too; and ended up having my stomach pumped and sitting with a psychiatrist who tried to tell me that I hated my mother.

The thing was, I didn't hate my mother. I never hated my mother. I pitied my mother. She wasn't a strong person, never had been. She was weak as a little child, and needed to be taken care of, that's all. So, I took over that role as well, during the years I still lived at home. I became the family's cook and housekeeper, and took care of my siblings as well. I wanted nothing more in the world than for my mother to love me as much as I loved her.

My biggest problem was that I hated me, so I couldn't really be angry at her for hating me, if that makes any sense. However, after that night, I never tried to kill myself again, mostly because

I'd been so terribly embarrassed to wake up and find that I'd messed that up as well, and with witnesses no less. By the way. I now praise God that He had other plans for me and didn't let me die.

You know, for many years I felt alone in my pain, thinking that everyone else's lives were wonderful and normal, whatever that meant. But I discovered, once I was grown, that there were many broken, abused, and hurting people in the world, who were just as messed up as I was, and who desperately needed help. Help that only knowing the love and Grace of Jesus could provide. I began to wonder if there was a way I could help people who were as troubled and damaged as I was, so I made myself available. Just listening at first, and later being more involved in ways that could help in the long term.

I can't say that finding out the world was full of suffering people was a comforting thought, but it did help me to understand human nature a bit more, and I didn't feel quite so alone. Churches are full of them, you know, row after row of pews filled with injured people. Many of those hurting people attended the church where my husband and I were established in ministry, and many of those who attended came to receive counseling. Before I knew it my office was the place to go, for folks needing an ear. Especially women who had suffered various types of abuse.

Once they'd heard my story, word got around and those women discovered they had a kindred spirit in me. Someone who might understand where they'd been, without giving them placating remarks and useless rhetoric. I discovered, in that time, that God can use absolutely anything. All of our pain, years of fear, desperation, doubt, guilt and shame. These experiences gave me an insight into their brand of suffering that some people probably wouldn't understand; and that no other life's experience could match. This made it possible for me to help them overcome their own darkness through the love of Christ. It also helped me forgive those who had hurt me. Because now I had discovered the true purpose for this pain.

The truth about guilt and shame is that they keep us from aggressively pursuing the Lord, because we feel unworthy of His love and forgiveness, and that is exactly what Satan is going for. Obviously, the worse he can make us feel about ourselves, the less we are going to believe God could ever truly love us. All I can say to that is: praise God for His Grace and mercy. Grace is that wonderful free gift He gives us when we don't deserve it, and mercy is the staving off of the eternal punishment we do deserve, just because He loves us. Isn't it wonderful that He doesn't just forgive us of our sin, but He frees us from all the guilt and shame of it at the very same time?

"For the scripture says, "Everyone who believes in Him will not be put to shame." Romans 10:11

And: *"There is therefore now no condemnation for those who are in Christ Jesus." Romans 8:1*

I love that this last scripture says, "There is therefore NOW no condemnation for those who are in Christ Jesus. In the Greek, emphasis is put on the word 'now', so that means wherever you are right now, at this moment, you are freed from condemnation, guilt and shame, as long as you are in Christ Jesus. Knowing that makes me smile. I don't deserve to be freed from my guilt and shame, but I am freed, nevertheless, because He loves me. And, because He has freed me from my sin and guilt, I am righteous, in Him. Not because of anything that I do, but because of His love and sacrifice for me. Praise God.

"For our sake He made Him to be sin, who knew no sin, so that in Him we might become the righteousness of God." 2Corinthians 5:21

These days, when I go through moments of guilt. And, believe me when I tell you that with this big mouth it happens more often than I would like to admit. I lean on the mercy of a God, whose love is hard to fathom, but always welcome.

"For I will be merciful toward their iniquities, and I will remember their sins no more." Hebrews 8:12

Remembering that I serve a God who does not condemn me for my mistakes, simply because I have chosen to trust Jesus as Savior, is magic to my soul.

"For God did not send His Son into the world to condemn the world, but in order that the world might be saved through Him." John 3:17

"In Him we have redemption through His blood, the forgiveness of our trespasses, according to the riches of His Grace." Ephesians 1:7

"If we confess our sins, He is faithful and just to forgive us our sins and to cleanse us from all unrighteousness." 1 John 1:9

Knowing that I am covered by His Grace is a wonderful gift. It fills me with a joy I can't explain. Perhaps I am so filled with joy, because once I was filled with so much pain. I don't know if everyone's experience with the redemptive power of Christ has been as overwhelming as mine, but mine is mind altering. A non-believer once asked me if I thought Jesus dying for my sins made me think I could do whatever I wanted without consequences. Cheap Grace, or a free pass to sin as much as I wanted, if you will. I couldn't believe the question. After everything He has done for me, I can't conceive of a world in which I would want to do anything to hurt Him.

Jesus has sacrificed so much for me, why would I want to take that gift and throw it back in His face? No, I will be grateful until the day I go to be with Him in heaven, and I will try my best every day, in His strength, to live in a faith filled way which will give Him all the glory He deserves. I would suffer and die for Him. He isn't just my Savior, He is my beloved heavenly Father (so much better than the flawed earthly father I had), and my Lord. And, I hope my life will always be an open book to the Holy Spirit. A tool He can use to draw others to the Kingdom of our God and King.

"Therefore, since we have been justified by faith, we have peace with God through our Lord Jesus Christ. Through Him we have also obtained access by faith into this grace in which we stand, and we rejoice in hope of the glory of God. More than that, we rejoice in our sufferings, knowing that suffering produces endurance, and endurance produces character, and

character produces hope, and hope does not put us to shame, because God's love has been poured out in our hearts through the Holy Spirit who has been given to us. For while we were still weak, at the right time Christ died for the ungodly. For one will scarcely die for a righteous person - though perhaps for a good person one would dare even to die - but God shows His love for us in that while we were still sinners, Christ died for us." Romans 5:1-8

And, now that my life is not filled with the guilt and shame that used to consume me and weigh me down day and night, I am free to live for Him. I am free to live a life of joy. I am free to be here for my husband, children, grandchildren and great grandchildren. I am free to write for His glory, to share the words He gives me to inscribe. I am free to share the

Gospel with everyone He puts in my path! And all of this because He has given me beauty for the ashes Satan had previously scattered over my life. Praise be to God!

"The Spirit of the Lord God is upon me, because the Lord has anointed me to bring good news to the poor; He has sent me to bind up the brokenhearted, to proclaim liberty to the captives, and the opening of the prison to those who are bound, to proclaim the year of the Lord's favor, and the day of vengeance of our God; to comfort all who mourn; to grant to those who mourn in Zion - to give them a crown of beauty instead of ashes, the oil of gladness instead of mourning, the garment of praise instead of a faint spirit; that they may be called oaks of righteousness, the planting of the Lord, that He may be glorified."
Isaiah 61:1-3

If anyone says, "I love God", and hates his brother, he is a liar; for he who does not love his brother whom he has seen cannot love God whom he has not seen.

1John 4:20

SATAN'S MANY NAMES —HATE

Hate is a harsh word, a despicable thought, and a destructive philosophy. And, if we are honest, we would most likely each have to admit we have felt hatred at some point in our lives. As much as I have always told my children, and my grand children, that they shouldn't even say the word, 'hate'. I admit that I have felt burning hatred toward other human beings.

I hated my biological father as a child. So much so that I used to wish him dead on a pretty regular basis. When he did die, years later, I felt the soul crushing guilt and blame. Thinking it was most surely due to all the times I had wished him dead over the years; that he died all alone, coughing his lungs up from the cancer which had eaten him from the inside out. By the time he died I had forgiven him for the abuse he'd inflicted on me as a child, but his death still haunted me.

I'd never experienced the father daughter relationship that so many women cherish, and I believe I was hoping beyond hope that since I was the one opening up and calling him to attempt reconciliation, he would be grateful for the opportunity to make amends and leap at the chance to make up for lost time. I tried to share Jesus with him then, when I called to talk to him and forgive him for the past, but he wasn't interested. Any more than he was interested in having a loving father daughter relationship with the offspring he'd abused. And, worst of all, he refused to acknowledge that abuse, as if perhaps he could convince me I'd been too young to have memories of anything like that, and that perhaps I was just believing some story my mom told me. I was almost ten when he went away to prison for heaven's sake.

I have to admit, though, looking back at the much younger me and my motives at the time (just about thirty years ago now), that I was probably calling him more for my own sake than for his. I knew by then that un-forgiveness was eating me alive. I've learned a lot about myself over the years. And, the younger me was not always so selfless as people may have thought. I do have to say the thought that he most likely died without knowing saving Grace ate at me for a very long time. And, I pray that the Lord came to him in those last moments. I wouldn't want him, or anyone for that matter, to have to endure hell for eternity.

I hated my ex-husband too. I don't anymore. As a matter of fact I led him to Christ after a serious back surgery, when he was vulnerable and open to listening to me for the first time in decades. We had been divorced for many years, and I am very happily married to the love of my life, Pastor Marty Young. But, I went to see him hoping he would be grateful for a visit. He was, as he hadn't received many. Marty was fine with it, simply because the man couldn't get up and move around yet, so he didn't have to worry about him trying to hurt me.

Several people asked me why I had cared to risk seeing him in order to share Jesus, after the years of physical, verbal and emotional abuse I'd received at his hands. In other words, why would I even care if this man went to hell when he died? Yet, deep inside, I knew he was only that person because he didn't know the love of Christ. Just as I had been a different person before that Grace and Love altered my life.

I have seen many people change in the wake of that love. I changed because of that love. And I felt that if I didn't share Christ's love with him, considering the people he usually associated with, he might never hear.

When I arrived, he was arguing with a nurse. It seemed he'd been doing a lot of that, and none of the nursing staff wanted to deal with him. I entered, he looked shocked (as I'd had a restraining order against him for decades before this) and I sat down. He got tears in his eyes and we talked. I took his hand and we prayed together. He received Christ as Savior that day, and my heart is so relieved to know that he is covered by the blood of Jesus.

Why did I care? I have discovered that hatred, and un-forgiveness, is like a cancer. It eats away at you and causes you to think, say and do things that you will be ashamed of later on. Satan is really fond of using hatred toward others as a way to break down our defenses.

As Christians we are commanded to love. Now, that doesn't mean we have to love everything the other person says and does, but it does mean we are supposed to love them through those times, just as Jesus loves us during the most unlovely times in our lives.

"Hatred stirs up strife, but love covers all offenses." Proverbs 10:12

I thought this would be an appropriate scripture to use, before going into the next segment of this chapter. I want to talk to you about the hatred and division currently going on in our country. I have always been a firm believer in an American citizen's right to free speech. And, I believe everyone is entitled to his, or her, own opinion. If I don't agree with you, so be it. If you don't agree with me, I can live with that. However, I have seen families destroyed, fist fights on the streets, innocent people attacked, and even killings committed, over political differences, in these recent years. What the heck is going on?

Satan is using hatred to create pandemonium. No matter our differences in opinion, we are still His, if we know Jesus as Savior. And we need to start treating others as we hope they would treat us. Let us be the beacon of light in an otherwise dark and demented world.

"So", you might ask, "should I never be angry"? To that I would say, even Jesus was angry sometimes. When he walked into the courtyard of the synagogue, for example, and saw the mess there.

"And Jesus entered the temple and drove out all who sold and bought in the temple, and He overturned the tables of the money-changers and the seats of those who sold pigeons. He said to them, "It is written, 'My house shall be called a house of prayer', but you make it a den of robbers."

Matthew 21:12-13

There is justifiable anger, and then there is anger just for the sake of it. Jesus was justified in his anger over the use of His Father's temple by greedy men. Can we say the same thing when we blow our cool over a child's messy accident, a spouse's mistake, a co-worker's wrong move, or even a car cutting us off in traffic? No, anger has become the norm for so many, and the use of angry words, foul language or violent actions just amplifies the situation. Things in this world in which we live have gotten completely out of hand. As Christians, we need to follow Paul's advice in Ephesians.

"Be angry and do not sin; do not let the sun go down on your anger, and give no opportunity to the devil." Ephesians 4:26-27

By succumbing to aggressive words or actions, in a fit of rage, we allow Satan to access our very emotions. And, I promise you, if you allow the devil to control your situation, you won't like the outcome. It isn't a far leap from anger to rage and hatred, which is why we see so many violent groups on the streets of American cities today, demolishing property and hurting people to make a point. Why has it become acceptable, in the eyes of some, to kill and destroy for the sake of their politics? That is one stage, it seems, where Satan has been granted unlimited access.

As followers of Christ, we are to be the peacemakers. That doesn't mean we shouldn't be involved in politics, or have opinions about: the way our country is being run; religious liberty; freedom of speech; our choice of political parties;

abortion policies; 2nd amendment rights; borders; walls; and all the other subjects floating around in the public square these days. Quite the contrary. If we don't step in and share our Christian views. If we don't make known our Christian standards and values in public, and vote our moral conscience. Then our country will become the godless wasteland for which some strive. No. Get involved, but be the voice of reason. We used to be able to voice our opinions without being physically attacked by opponents. Let's be the ones that reach for unity of purpose past party lines. Listen, and don't be angry. It is okay to disagree, but, disagree agreeably.

"Know this, my beloved brothers; let every person be quick to hear, slow to speak, slow to anger; for the anger of a man does not produce the righteousness of

God." James 1:19-20

I've often heard people say they can't control their anger; that they just are who they are and that isn't going to change; or, that everyone in their family has an anger problem, so they come by it honestly. I've even heard that their parents were like that, so they don't have a choice. Well, you do have a choice. If you choose Jesus, He will work on you, fill your heart with peace and help you overcome the need to have the last word. The need to exact revenge and calm the feelings of hate that bubble up inside until they burst forth in a fit of temper.

No power in the world is stronger than the power of Love. You can use it to conquer the enemy, to make your point, to triumph in war, to win souls, to calm hearts and to control your own racing mind. Jesus is Love. Let Him direct your paths. Be the person who breaks down spiritual walls, in the name of our Lord .

"But I say to you who hear, Love your enemies, do good to those who hate you, bless those who curse you, pray for those who abuse you. To one who strikes you on the cheek, offer the other also, and from one who takes away your cloak do not withhold your tunic either. Give to everyone who begs from you, and from one who takes away your goods do not demand them back. And as you wish that others would do to you, do so to them.

"If you love those who love you, what benefit is that to you? For even sinners love those who love them. And if you do good to those who do good to you, what benefit is that to you? For even sinners do the same. And if you lend to those from whom

you expect to receive, what credit is that to you? Even sinners lend to sinners to get back the same amount. But love your enemies, and do good, and lend, expecting nothing in return, and your reward will be great, and you will be sons of the Most High, for He is kind to the ungrateful and the evil. Be merciful, even as your Father is merciful." Luke 6:27-36

I guess that pretty well covers that!

I have a bit of a Grandma story to interject here. My granddaughter and I were talking one day and she said, "Grandma, I know we have Jesus in our hearts, so we're supposed to be nice to everyone. But, that doesn't mean we should be nice to the bad guys, does it? You know, the ones that are really mean?"

I asked her who the bad guys were, and she said, " Well, people who do bad stuff."

I had to chuckle at that. I told her that, in that case, we are all bad guys. We all do 'bad stuff' sometimes. That is why Jesus died to take our sin upon Himself. He did it to save every last one of us from our bad stuff; if we choose to trust and believe in Him; so we can be in heaven with Him when we die. She looked at me, and her eyes got huge. "Oh, I never thought of it like that." She said.

It's easy to assign degrees of good and bad, if we aren't careful. Thinking ourselves more holy than someone else. Figuring one sin worse than another, or better than some. But, in God's Holy eyes, sin is sin, as simple as that. Nope, none of us is righteous without the sacrifice of Jesus. His selfless act covered it all.

"As it is written: None is righteous, no, not one; no one understands; no one seeks for God. All have turned aside; together they have become worthless; no one does good, not even one." Romans 3:10-12

I explained to her that sometimes, all we can do is be nice to those people who aren't very nice. Even if they are mean to us first. Peace has to start somewhere. Let it begin with me.

"If your enemy is hungry, give him bread to eat, and if he is thirsty, give him water to drink, for you will heap burning coals on his head, and the Lord will reward you." Proverbs 25:21-22

And this, my friends, is what they call 'killing them with kindness'.

Don't let Satan win with hate. We who are 'His', should be filling the world with Love!

Who is wise and understanding among you? By his good conduct let him show his works in the meekness of wisdom. But if you have bitter jealousy and selfish ambition in your hearts, do not boast and be false to the truth. This is not the wisdom that comes down from above, but is earthly, unspiritual, demonic. For where jealousy and selfish ambition exist, there will be disorder and every vile practice. But the wisdom from above is first pure, then peaceable, gentle, open to reason, full of mercy and good fruits, impartial and sincere.

James 3:13-17

SATAN'S MANY NAMES —ENVY AND JEALOUSY

I would like to say firstly that envy and jealousy are mindsets that can run rampant in many areas of our lives. And, though some people associate them only with matters of the heart, their resulting damage certainly is not limited to thwarted romance. This evil duo can breed and flourish in our finances, or lack thereof; our career and work lives; our various relationships; and our worship and ownership of personal possessions, just to name a few. This idea of being envious or jealous of what someone else has, is not new by any means. After all, God did add it to the 'big ten' for a reason. "*You shall not covet your neighbor's house, you shall not covet your neighbor's wife, or his male servant, or his female servant, or his ox, or his donkey, or anything that is your neighbor's. Exodus 20:17* And, yes, you are right, coveting is wanting something that belongs to someone else. But, it can also include thinking that you deserve it more than they, and being resentful that they are being blessed, when you might feel you are not as blessed as you would like to be.

When I was a girl, I was always very envious of my older sister, Dawn. Sadly, she passed away at only thirty three years of age, leaving behind a very young son, Tim. Dawn was a beauty. The kind of drop dead gorgeous girl who left men with their mouths hanging open when she walked by. But, because we weren't brought up around particularly good, or Christian, influences most of our lives, she got terribly off track, in a world filled with alcohol, sex and drugs.

She had finally started to come around, before her life was tragically cut short, and gave her heart to Jesus. But, the unthinkable happened when she mixed prescription medications with alcohol. I think of her often, and mourn the fact that she didn't get to see her beautiful son grow up to be the good man he is today. Because of the way she left things, he had to go through a lot of heartache and trouble to get where he is currently.

When I was about eleven, and Dawn was around fourteen-ish, I remember watching her put on makeup one day. I sat enthralled, as she applied mascara to her long, thick lashes, pouted her lips to add color, and then sat in front of the mirror practicing her assorted sexy, enticing looks for all the boy's entertainment later (I know, I know, She was only 14, but I told you we weren't brought up in the best of circumstances; and Dawn actually started seeing men at 12 years old, so she was pretty experienced by the age in this story.). I desperately wanted to be like her; and I always wondered why she was so beautiful, and I was so, well, average.

One day I asked my mother if I was pretty. Her answer; which will always occupy that small part of my brain where little girls go when they need encouragement; was, "Don't worry about being pretty. There are other things more important than pretty." Thereby filling my encouragement place with the very real fact that I would never be much to look at. Now, she never did tell me what those 'more important' things were, or if I possessed any of them, but at least I knew I'd never have to worry about wasting time entering beauty contests.

I was forever pestering my sister to share her beauty secrets with me, but alas, it seemed for the most part that she was a natural beauty, and had no huge secrets to reveal. Some people have it and some people don't. Or, at least that was the story she was pedaling.

One day I walked into the bathroom after my sister had just walked out, and I saw an unfamiliar small bottle on the vanity top. I wondered if it was some secret beauty potion. I removed the lid and smelled. There really wasn't much of an aroma.

I dipped my pinky into the liquid and tasted. It was a bit salty, but didn't have any flavor. I just knew it was Dawn's secret. I wet a tissue with the solution and rubbed it all over my face. Then I stuck my tongue in the bottle, tasted again, and hastily drank the remainder of the bottle, burying the empty container deep in the garbage bin. I left the bathroom, and readied myself for the bus, just knowing that by the time I got out of school that day, I would be ravishingly beautiful.

As I was about to walk out the front door, my mom walked into the bathroom. She quickly came back out and said, "Has anyone seen my urine sample? It was on the vanity top. I have a doctor's appointment today and I can't find it in the bathroom."

I never did tell my mom what happened to

her urine sample. I didn't die from drinking it, but I sure felt like I should have. I've told my husband, my kids and my grandkids about most of the stupid things I did when I was young, so of course they all know about the time I drank my mom's pee and they got a good laugh out of the story. I find it amusing to recount today. However, at the same time my heart aches for that jealous little girl who never felt pretty or loved. Envy, and jealousy, can cause us to do some pretty stupid things.

Probably the saddest thing was this. Two nights before my sister's death years later she called me at about 2:00a.m. She had been drinking and was grieving over the years of her life she'd wasted partying. She was feeling pretty badly about some of those especially evil things she'd done in the drunk and high moments of her youth. Things that had negatively affected me, our sisters Robin, and Bobbi, and our brother Rick. I reminded her that none of us is perfect, but that isn't her fault. And, that she had Jesus as Savior now, so the minute she'd asked for forgiveness, He had forgiven her. I told her I loved her, and had forgiven her long ago; and she proceeded to tell me that she had always been very jealous of me.

I was floored by that confession and told her she must have me confused with someone else, because I'd always been envious of her. She then went on to tell me that in her life all she ever really had, or indeed even thought important, was her looks. And, that now as she was getting older, those were going the way of all outer beauty, so she didn't think of them as so great anymore.

She told me she knew I'd always wanted to be beautiful on the outside like her; that basically I'd wanted to be her; but that I had something much better than superficial beauty. She told me I was beautiful on the inside, and that no amount of time could fade true inner beauty. She told me that inner beauty grew, while outer beauty wilted and died away. Then she told me she'd always dreamed of being me when she grew up, and we laughed together. Turned out that my big sister was probably a little smarter, and more spiritually attuned, than I'd ever thought.

Two nights later I got a call. Dawn had gone into the doctor for antibiotics earlier that day. Her doctor was aware of her history with drugs and alcohol. He told her she absolutely could not drink while on these medications. She went home, took her meds and poured herself a good stiff drink. A few minutes later she passed out and fell, hitting her head on the base of her shower. We were all called to be by her side; which for Robin and I was half a country away; where we discovered that the doctors had already pronounced her brain dead.

We were shocked, when we arrived at the hospital, to see what had become of the physically beautiful woman we knew. Her head was shaved; and her body, from head to toe, so swollen that she was entirely unrecognizable. Doctors had tried to relieve the swelling on her brain, but the surgery left her face and head so bruised and distorted, she almost didn't look human. We were told there was no brain function, and that they would be turning off life support later that day. We held her hands and said goodbye. It was all so sad and very surreal.

I know my sister is in the arms of Jesus, and that I will see her again one day. She is forgiven and free, and she is beautiful inside and out.

"A tranquil heart gives life to the flesh, but envy makes the bones rot." Proverbs 14:30

Have you ever worked a job where you always seemed to be picking up the slack for another employee who shirked their duties? Yep, me too.

Have you ever had a job where you worked your fingers to the bone, and a co-worker who was not willing to put in the time or sweat came to you, over and over, to bemoan the fact that you seem to get all the 'lucky' breaks? You know, like promotions and raises? Yes.

And then there's the co-worker who; without your knowledge, and behind your back; takes credit for your work, and ends up getting the raise or promotion you were working for. That's a gut wrenching one.

Or, perhaps you are that someone, who wants the best, but isn't willing to do the hard work it takes to earn the best? Perhaps attempting to profit from someone else's labor?

We often work with others who envy our work ethic, but can't seem to get it together enough to develop a good work ethic of their own. Sometimes that person's envy builds to a point that they lie to take credit for your work, or tell untruths in order to cause you trouble, because your very existence in the work place is a threat to them. I actually worked a job in a window factory once where a group of union employees (I wasn't in the union), came to me and told me to quit working so hard, because I was making them look bad. I didn't change my work habits and came outside after work one day to find four flat tires.

I've had experience with several of these types. But, one that stands out in my mind was the co-worker who would leave me to do all the work; while she went home each and every single day with a 'migraine'. Then she would make her way back in for a few minutes after 10:00p.m. Mind you, this was after I had just left for the day, exhausted from twelve to sixteen grueling hours. She would then send out emails to managers, giving them the impression she'd been there for all those many hours working her tail off.

I didn't know this was going on until I began to receive emails from higher ups on the corporate food chain, telling me I needed to step up to the plate and help this gal more, since she was obviously working herself half to death being there so late every night. Yep, she even earned a most valuable supervisor of the year award that year, from those same higher ups, and was promoted before I was. At that point I was very envious of her luck, and absolutely did not think she deserved any of those accolades. My thoughts were black with jealousy, which certainly wasn't helping anything.

You might think she got away with murder. I suppose to a certain extent she did. But, after she was promoted to the position, which could have been mine, she didn't know what in the world she was doing. You see, she had always left the work to me, so she had no clue how to do even the simplest of reports for our department. To cover for herself she began to squirrel away all the paperwork she received from the statistics department in her desk drawers. It built up and stacked up, until there was simply no saving her. I had continued to do my job, of course, so that part of the department was doing fine, but her responsibilities were left undone until corporate finally wanted to know what the heck was going on.

You know, as jealous as I felt and as wrong as the entire situation was, if she had come to me I would have helped her. I know that sounds stupid, but I don't carry grudges and I don't like to see anyone fail. I had no idea at that time that she was so far behind and that she had no clue as to how to do her job. I guess she was probably too embarrassed to come to me, since she had beaten me out of that very position, to tell me she didn't know how to do the job.

By the time any real investigation started she had already done some shopping around. With her stellar, falsified, work record she was able to land a position, with the same company no less, at another center location. Receiving a huge promotion and pay raise as a nice cherry on top.

The company sent in someone to figure out what had gone wrong. They found all the months and months of neglected statistics and unfinished reports in her desk drawers, and pretty quickly figured out what had happened. I got my promotion and the department excelled.

Down the road, people at the new center figured out her game and she was fired. Actually, at that point I felt a little sorry for her. Her jealousy and envy left her to ride another's coat tails until she was completely undone.

And, though she had no one to blame but herself, many careers were sidelined, or derailed, in the process. Envy can cause us to do some pretty despicable things. But, I too had been bitten by the jealousy bug and her success at my expense had cost me my peace for many months. So, I certainly wasn't any better. This is why we are supposed to turn things over to the Lord. He is our justifier.

We are all confronted by situations where someone we know is blessed and we have a choice. We can be glad for them, or we can be jealous.

Thinking, "Why should they get that and not me? Why would God bless them so much and I feel like I am never equally blessed? What makes them so special?" Envy, jealousy, the old green eyed monster, or Satan if you will, is a divider. He is a liar, and he will destroy families, businesses, churches, and friendships with jealousy and envy. Don't get sucked into that void. When you see a friend, family member, or colleague blessed, be happy for them. Congratulate them. It will make you both feel better.

"Do not be overcome by evil, but overcome evil with good." Romans 12:21

When pride comes, then comes disgrace,
but with the humble is wisdom.

        Proverbs 11:2

SATAN'S MANY NAMES —PRIDE AND ARROGANCE

First off, let me say that there is Pride, and then there is PRIDE. Or to put it a little differently: There is nothing wrong with being proud of your children and grand children, a job well done, or overcoming an obstacle. As long as we acknowledge that God is the giver of all good gifts and that, *"I can do all things through Him who strengthens me." Philippians 4:13*

The problem comes when we mix pride and arrogance. I am all too aware of the devastating effects of this deadly combination, due to the fact that it was once prevalent in my own personal and professional life.

Growing up the way I did, abused, and then taking on the responsibility of caring for my siblings and our household, I grew very independent, or self-dependent if you will. But, this wasn't a healthy independence. It certainly wasn't a dependence centered in the Lord. I just figured I could do it all on my own. I knew I couldn't count on anyone else, and as far as I was concerned that included God. So, my attitude became very arrogant and self sufficient.

Now, don't get me wrong. A certain amount of self sufficiency is good. We need to be able to take care of our own affairs, such as: working a job, paying our bills, household chores, and personal hygiene, but to assume we have the power to direct our own path and not need input and guidance from the Father, is a very haughty and superior attitude indeed. Well, I have to tell you honestly, I had that one down pretty well.

As a kid I was defiant, but shy and unsure of my place in the universe. I excelled in school and was often called precocious, but, due to treatment at home and bullying from other children, thought quite often of killing myself. As I grew into adulthood, I was still terribly insecure, though I covered it up with an attitude of outward self assurance which was completely false, but believable. I absolutely would not ever ask anyone for help, or accept help if someone offered. Though I believe, looking back, that several of those people offering assistance had been sent by the Lord to direct me.

I managed a number of businesses over the

years, even taking on a couple that were failing, and successfully turning them around. I wasn't afraid to get my hands dirty, but I was very bossy. The people who worked for me knew I would do anything for them, but I expected them to be loyal to me and me alone. I got to the point where I felt almost indestructible, and certainly completely indispensible. And let me tell you, no human being on this earth is either. By the time I married Marty and studied for my minister's license I was feeling, if falsely, pretty confident in 'me'. I wasn't giving any of the credit to Jesus; the one who had seen me through that terrible childhood, and those first two disastrous marriages. Instead, accepting plenty of credit for myself for what I'd accomplished. After all (I reasoned), I had worked hard my whole life, hadn't I? Why should anyone else get credit? Especially God, the one who had stood back and let me suffer all those years.

Can I tell you. God will not allow anyone to steal His glory forever. As the Pastor's wife, I became very knowledgeable in scripture. I memorized and memorized, but none of it, not a bit, ever made it from my head to my heart. I was living a lie. I was a horror to live with and I ruled with an iron fist at home and at the church where we ministered. My prayers were long soliloquies, of meaningless babbling.

I once heard a random person say, "Don't follow someone who has memorized all the scriptures. Follow someone who lives by the scriptures." I would not have been that person to follow. But God....... Here we go again. But

God stepped into my life and turned everything upside down.

Some might say that God abandoned me, and that this was why I got cancer. I believe that God used cancer to get my attention. Apart from Him, I was becoming more and more lost in my own arrogance and PRIDE. Going nowhere, spiritually, fast. When He allowed cancer to invade my body (and let's face it, nothing happens that doesn't first go through the hands of the Father), He guided me to a path of Faith in Him, that would lead me back to life.

Even if I hadn't been healed of cancer by His mighty hand, through the power of Jesus' sacrifice, I still would have been better off than I was before, because throughout it all He remained by my side and I recognized His presence as I never had before. I learned more about Him and more about me than I'd ever known. I discovered that I could always count on His Grace, His Love, and His protection.

Once I began to recognize God's presence in my life and became confident in Him, my self-absorption and misplaced self-sufficiency turned into God sufficiency. I became a more compassionate person, and I wanted to share the knowledge of this new understanding of Grace that He had given Marty and I with everyone I met. So no one would ever have to feel the emptiness I'd lived with for so many years.

Now, I'm not going to try to tell you I am never bossy anymore, or that I never ramble. That would be a lie. Some habits are harder to break than others. But, I will tell you that now when I read the Word, I read it with my heart and not my head. And my prayers are no longer incessant, fake babbling. You see, I know that God heals. I am living, breathing proof that through the power of Jesus' life, death and resurrection, He embodies all the power of the universe and beyond. He is healer, He is provider, He is rescuer. He is helper, He is Lord, He is mighty to save. He is my everything.

"Everyone who is arrogant in heart is an abomination to the Lord; be assured, he will not go unpunished." Proverbs 16:5

I believe if I had continued on the path I was following before God allowed cancer to come into my life. If I had refused His helping hand and this new revelation of Grace. If I had continued to try and do it on my own, without reaching out to His healing power. I would be dead. Yet, here I am to praise His Holy Name!

I also believe God had plans for me. Books to write; a husband to grow old with; grand children to cuddle and teach; Love to share; and the Gospel to shout to the nations. By choosing to accept His path and guidance, I am forever blessed.

"The pride of your heart has deceived you, you who live in the clefts of the rock, in your lofty dwelling, who say in your heart, "Who will bring me down to the ground?" Obadiah 1:3

Having come from a history of abuse. One that culminated in an unhealthy sense of self sufficiency. Which then morphed into arrogance and stubborn pride. I have to say that those traits are easier to spot in others as well. Sometimes quite uncomfortably so. I have met pastors, and pastor's wives who are, sadly, more interested in how 'holy' they appear to others, (on the surface), than how they treat people and how well their congregations are doing.

I'm not trying to be disparaging here. There are plenty of good, caring pastors out there as well. We are friends with many of them. But, in a broken world, which is divided and hurting; any ministers who are more concerned with their own level of comfort, than the well being of their church, are not doing anything to mend the horrific rift in our society. Instead, they are letting their pride dictate their treatment, or mistreatment, of others. And let's face it, church is not just a building and the pews therein. The 'Church' is followers of Christ going wherever God sends them in search of hurting people needing His Grace.

A minister's wife was standing in front of me and my grand children one day at McDonalds. It was cold outside and a homeless man made his way inside for warmth. This woman and her pastor husband were well known in the community for their prominent billboards and television commercials talking about the welcoming nature of their church and church family. The homeless man saw her, and his face lit up in recognition. He approached her. But as she turned from the counter and saw him, her face screwed up in disgust. She took a step back and hissed, "Get away from me, right this minute. You are filthy." The hurt on his face was immediate and intense, but she didn't seem to be phased by that. I was shocked. We bought an extra cheeseburger and fries, and invited the stranger to sit with us. He smiled and looked relieved. A homeless Viet Nam Veteran, he regaled us with stories as we ate, and the grandkids listened raptly to every word he said.

The gentleman thanked us as we were parting to go our separate ways. And, he said, "I appreciate your kindness. That woman embarrassed me so badly, I wasn't sure what I was going to do next. I guess I thought she would be different, you know, because she's a famous minister's wife and all. It's nice to know there are still people out here who care."

That exchange between the minister's wife and a stranger ate at me for weeks. We are supposed to be Jesus to those we meet. We are supposed to be His hands and feet in an imperfect world. When we allow false pride and judgmental arrogance to dictate our actions, we murder the spirits of those around us. There is not one of us any better than another. Where is the compassion that used to separate God's people from the rest of the world?

I believe God calls us to reject pride and reach out to those who do not yet know Him. We are to be not only His hands and feet to the world, but His heart as well.

"For I was hungry and you gave me food, I was thirsty and you gave me drink, I was a stranger and you welcomed me, I was naked and you clothed me, I was sick and you visited me, I was in prison and you came to me. Then the righteous will answer him, saying, 'Lord, when did we see you hungry and feed you, or thirsty and give you a drink? And when did we see you a stranger and welcome you,

or naked and clothe you? And when did we see you sick or in prison and visit you?' And the King will answer them, "Truly, I say to you, as you did it to one of the least of these, my brothers, you did it to me". Matthew 25:35-40

"For by the grace given to me I say to everyone among you not to think of himself more highly than he ought to think, but to think with sober judgment, each according to the measure of faith that God has assigned." Romans 12:3

"Scoffer is the name of the arrogant, haughty man who acts with arrogant pride." Proverbs 21:24

To see the pain of the world is a difficult thing, especially as a Christian. For we know the answer to that pain is the joy of the Lord, if only those who so desperately need Him would let Him in. To minister to those in pain is a noble thing, even when it brings suffering. For sharing the Gospel is our goal and our command. To give of ourselves for the Kingdom, is to welcome the freedom of Christ, in hopes that others will see the marvelous gift of our Savior.

Let us put away our selfish pride, our haughty arrogance and our self-centeredness. Let us help one another to be the family of Christ He desires, and the grateful distributors of His cleansing Grace.

"But He gives more Grace. Therefore it says, God opposes the proud, but gives Grace to the humble. Submit yourselves therefore to God. Resist the devil, and he will flee from you. Draw near to God, and He will draw near to you. Cleanse your hands you sinners, and purify your hearts, you double minded." James 4:6-8

We are afflicted in every way, but not crushed; perplexed, but not driven to despair; persecuted, but not forsaken; struck down, but not destroyed; always carrying in the body the death of Jesus, so that the life of Jesus may also be manifested in our bodies.

2 Corinthians 4:8-10

SATAN'S MANY NAMES —GRIEF AND DESPAIR

Grief and Despair; different, yet so often, sadly, going hand in hand. Grief is deep sorrow, especially as the result of a death; and is a necessary step in proper healing. Despair, on the other hand, is the complete absence of hope. As Christians, we know that to be absent from the body, is to be present with the Lord, so hope is never abandoned. But, to an unbeliever, death isn't merely deep sorrow; it is great and unbearable loss. A loss they, in many cases, cannot fathom living through.

When an individual doesn't believe in an

eternity with the Living God, sorrow takes a further step that evolves into hopelessness. With no hope of an eternity with Jesus, despair can overwhelm those who are weak among us. This is one of the many reasons we must strive to share the truth of the Gospel with everyone we meet. I too was once without hope, searching for a reason to continue. It is not a good place to be. My greatest desire is to make sure no one I meet ever has to live in a similar deep pit of despair.

When my baby son died, of SIDS, at almost eight months old, I was devastated and entirely devoid of hope. Due to the circumstances in my own childhood, I didn't have faith that God loved me, or wanted to protect me. I also wasn't sure where my baby had gone, or if I would ever see him again. Today I praise God that I already had a son, Aaron, who was four years old at that time. His life, and his presence in mine, gave me a reason to live. Sadly, my faith then was so small that if Aaron had not been around to offer me a reason for living, I am sure I would have taken my own life. It saddens me to think I had such little regard for the Lord, and I'm sure my faithlessness caused Him great pain too. Thankfully, I know now how much I am loved, and I faithfully depend on Him every day.

I still remember clearly the morning I found my infant son dead in his crib. Stepping over the threshold, into his room, I felt the cold as it attempted to burrow into my bones. I knew, before I knew, and I was deathly afraid to approach his bed. As I did, I saw that he lay with his eyes open and his arms outstretched, a look of peace on his face, as if he was waiting to be picked up. I sobbed and obliged. Holding him tight to my chest, I ran.

Looking back now, it was clear if I'd been looking. I know he was transported in the arms of angels. I know he is safely in the hands of Jesus, and that his transition from life to death was serene. However, all those details escaped me then, when in a moment of panic I rushed outside and began screaming for help.

I remember a neighbor, a self professing Jehovah's Witness, walking up to me in the street that day and telling me that my baby was dead because I was not a Jehovah's Witness. He told me that because, like pagans, we celebrate Christmas and birthdays, God had punished me by taking my child away. In my absolute grief and sorrow,

I took everything he said and absorbed it into my being. I knew then that it was all my fault. I was the reason my son died. I deserved the pain I was feeling and I could never be forgiven. I lived with the guilt of my son's death for many years, believing what that man had told me on the morning of my tragedy. I just never knew what to do about it.

I walked around in a fog for days. Aaron's needs were my only concern. I couldn't think any further than that. On the morning of the funeral, in January, the weather was beautiful. It made me angry to see people smiling; to feel the sun on my cheeks and the breeze in my hair. How dare they be happy, when we were about to bury my baby in the ground?

The white casket looked impossibly small.

Jackie was surrounded by soft, white satin, and held a tiny teddy bear. His face was waxen, and I immediately regretted touching him, as the feel of his skin would haunt me for years. As the funeral director closed the ornately, tufted lid of the coffin, my heart began to race and I thought I would die right then and there. We made our way to the cemetery. A chill in the air reminded it was winter, but birds still chirped and sang in the trees, causing me to grit my teeth and clench my fists.

Rows upon rows of graves, some dating back to the beginning of the previous century and before, cast shadows on the ground; and told the stories of lives which had ended on this earthly plane; until we came upon a freshly dug hole partially covered in green indoor-outdoor carpet.

A minister I'd never met, and who was probably arranged by my mother-in-law, rambled for an indeterminate amount of time. And then, the workmen lowered the small white box into the earth. I crumbled into myself.

That event, in minutest detail, is engrained in my memory. And the months that followed, with Satan attacking me on every front, filling my heart with despair, will forever remind me of that time in my life when I did not have the faith to believe. Yes, Satan worked on me daily. Depression ate at me. A sense of shame, for being a terrible mother who allowed her child to die, filled me with guilt and pain. I was not just grieving, I was buried in a despair so deep I couldn't see my way out. I longed to be dead. And, if it had not been for Aaron, I would have been.

Eventually, after a few years, the searing pain diminished some. Though the thought of Jackie and his death would resurface and bring me to tears at the oddest times, and continued throughout the years until, much later, when I gave myself and my grief wholeheartedly to Jesus.

Satan is evil, and he is a liar. He will use whatever power we give him to destroy us. For decades, I allowed him to drown me in grief. No more. I am no longer wrapped in despair in the arms of Satan. I know now to give everything over to my Lord and healer.

"Why are you cast down, O my soul, and why are you in turmoil within me? Hope in God; for I shall again praise Him, my salvation and my God." Psalm 43:5

"I waited patiently for the Lord; He inclined to

me and heard my cry. He drew me up from the pit of destruction, out of the miry bog, and set my feet upon a rock, making my steps secure." Psalm 40:1-2

The loss of my sister, followed a week later by my mom, was very difficult. I grieved over the fact that both of their deaths were drug and alcohol related, and I felt I had failed to make much of a difference in their lives, always wondering why I couldn't have done more. The death of my biological father was hard on me for a different reason. There had been so much hate for him in my younger years that I felt guilty when he died a horrible death. I Wondered if all the years of wishing him dead had culminated in his demise. And, in this case I honestly felt bad that I didn't hurt very much in regard to his passing.

My biggest concern for him was whether or

not he had given his life to Christ before he died. I suppose I will never know that until I am with Jesus. Satan worked on me nonstop. Guilt over my motives when I'd called him to seek amends, and my not so stellar intentions of being the 'bigger' person, which had in turn led to his anger and denial. No wonder I continued to live in brokenness for so many years.

God has healed my heart about so many things, and I am very grateful. But, I want others to know that they do not have to allow Satan to interject his evil into their lives. They do not have to allow him to take their already difficult season, and compound it with his lies and hate. By allowing Jesus to sooth their hearts and take their pain, they can be in a position of peace.

I have a friend who was very angry with her

father. She claimed some disturbing things similar to instances from my own childhood. Unlike my own biological father, who declared atheism until he died, her father had given his life to Christ in his later years. My husband and I encouraged her to seek peace with him. To forgive him. Explaining to her that un-forgiveness is much harder on the person who refuses to forgive, than it is on the person they are refusing to forgive.

I once heard it put this way: Refusing to forgive is like drinking poison and expecting the other person to fall down dead. She didn't want to hear my pleas, or the pleas of my husband, and subsequently, years marched on. Her father died, and at the funeral she was a basket case. Her guilt at not approaching him in forgiveness; even though, just like my father, he hadn't asked for it; consumed her. Her grief and despair were unrelenting, and caused her much unhealed pain. Not because God wouldn't have healed her if she'd asked, but because she refused to ask Him.

She later acquired some bad habits that have caused her major health problems over the years, and it is sad to see her afflicted in so many ways. Grief, which has morphed into despair is an ugly thing. Forgiveness is necessary in overcoming many of Satan's traps. Learn to forgive. Even if you think someone else started it, and you feel they should be asking you for forgiveness. Forgive, even if you think they don't deserve it. Remember, we didn't deserve it either. Take my word for it. Forgiveness is very freeing.

God can heal your grief. He will comfort you and wipe away your tears. Come to Him when it seems that all is lost. Because, 'All is Lost' is just one more lie of the devil. Jesus is a way maker, and a grief taker. Trust Him.

"The Lord is near to the brokenhearted and saves the crushed in spirit." Psalm 34:18

"Blessed are those who mourn, for they shall be comforted." Matthew 5:4

"He heals the brokenhearted and binds up their wounds." Psalm 147:3

"He will wipe away every tear from your eyes, and death shall be no more, neither shall there be mourning, nor crying, nor pain anymore, for the former things have passed away." Revelation 21:4

For while we were still weak, at the right time Christ died for the ungodly.

                                        Romans 5:6

SATAN'S MANY NAMES —HELPLESSNESS AND HOPELESSNESS

First I would like to say that I no longer feel helpless and hopeless. I am aware this is due to the fact that I know Jesus has my back. What a relief to know we serve a God who is able and willing to protect and defend, heal, and make us whole.

I am no longer filled with insecurity and self hatred, the way I was for the first five and a half decades of my life. I realize now that I don't have to be good enough on my own. God created me and knows exactly who I am. He is perfect, and

He loves me. He is my justifier.

"But He said to me, "My Grace is sufficient for you, for my power is made perfect in weakness." 2 Corinthians 12:9

I tried so hard, as a young person, to be my own strength. It didn't work. Over and over I proved only one thing; that I messed it all up, that I couldn't do it on my own. I was weak, and ashamed in my weakness. But, that was because I didn't know I was supposed to turn it all over to Jesus and let Him be my strength. I hated myself and I hated my insecurities. But He loved me anyway. Now I know.

"Not that I am speaking of being in need, for I have learned in whatever situation I am to be content. I know how to be brought low, and I know how to abound. In any and every circumstance, I

have learned the secret of facing plenty and hunger, abundance and need. I can do all things through Christ who strengthens me." Philippians 4:11-13

All those years that I spent hating myself. What a waste of His time and mine. I was too ashamed to approach Him and admit I was a miserable sinner, to ask for His help, as if He didn't already know those things anyway. So, I went about my life trying to make people think I was capable; that I had it all together; that I was someone they could count on. When in reality, I was nothing but a huge inglorious mess. However, God can see through all the self hatred and insecurity. We only have to admit that we are sinners and that we need Him. What a relief.

"If we confess our sins, He is faithful and just to forgive us our sins and to cleanse us from all

unrighteousness. If we say we have not sinned, we make Him a liar, and His Word is not in us." 1 John 1:9,10

I spent way too many years hung up on outward beauty. Or, well, the fact that I didn't believe I had any. I assumed I was just as lacking on the inside, as I'd always believed myself to be lacking on the outside. But God can use us even when we don't feel very useful. He sees us from an entirely different perspective.

"But the Lord said to Samuel, "Do not look on his appearance or on the height of his stature, because I have rejected him. For the Lord sees not as man sees: man looks on the outward appearance, but the Lord looks on the heart." 1 Samuel 16:7

I spent those decades believing that if I didn't take care of myself, no one would. I pretended to the world that I was entirely self-sufficient, when in fact I was nothing but an insecure little girl. Now I am secure in Christ. I can do nothing without Him, but He makes me capable through His love and compassion. I no longer worry about how I will get by. Instead I seek Him; His love; His Grace; His abundance.

"Therefore do not be anxious, saying, "What shall we eat?" or "What shall we drink?" or "What shall we wear?" For the Gentiles seek after all these things, and your Heavenly Father knows that you need them all. But seek first the Kingdom of God and His righteousness, and all these things will be added to you." Matthew 6: 31-33

Once I began to witness the Love of Christ in action in my own life. I wanted to share Him with others. How could I ever receive so great a gift, and not share it? That would be like having the cure for cancer, and not rushing to the cancer center to feed it to everyone who suffers. However, as my husband and I have discovered over the years, not everyone is so eager to know Him. Not everyone is so eager for the cure. Just as I had thought, for so many years, that He didn't care about me. There seemed to be many hurting people, that for a variety of reasons, had those same false delusions. I knew I just had to tell them my story, and that perhaps it would cause them to want to hear more of His love. He took it from there.

"O Lord, You hear the desire of the afflicted; You will strengthen their heart; You will incline Your ear to do justice to the fatherless and the oppressed, so that man who is of the earth may strike terror no

more." Psalm 10:17,18

As I began to follow the Lord I wondered if I would be strong enough to endure if persecution happened. I wondered if God would be there to dig me out if I became buried in self doubt once again. Would I stand strong, or would I capitulate under pressure? I discovered, the hard way, that God was always with me and would keep me strong.

I began working a job for a large airline. While in training, one of my co-workers discovered I was a minister's wife. Shortly thereafter I was called to human resources and told, in no uncertain terms, that I would not be allowed to proselytize in the work place, and then I was accused of saying something I had not said. I protested, but was put on a warning. I already knew, as it was plainly stated in the company policy booklet assigned at the beginning of training, that soliciting of any kind was not permitted. And, I had no plans to do anything on 'their' time that would cause trouble. I was upset though, that I was being accused of saying something unkind about a co-worker, as I don't do that sort of thing.

I was great at my job, and doing very well with the company. I had already won several awards for accomplishments in the work place.

What the company considered my 'second' offence, was a conversation with a customer. The customer had recently lost her husband and asked me if I was a Christian. I indicated that I was and she asked me to pray with her. Perhaps I shouldn't have, but I figured since the customer had initiated the conversation, I couldn't be held responsible. I began to pray with her and a supervisor came behind me and kicked the back of my chair so hard I was thrown out onto the carpet. I know, I know, I probably should have refused to pray with my customer, but I am the Pastor's wife after all.

Then there was the third occurrence. One day a young gay man came to me with questions. Apparently, he had heard I was a minister's wife and was seeking advice. I had not approached him in any way. We were in the break room, on our own time, so I thought there would be no harm in answering his questions. We had several such meetings, always initiated by him, and always in the break room. I was happy to help him discover more of the Lord in a loving and non-judgmental way, as long as I was operating within company guidelines.

After one of these meetings the young man asked me if I would be willing to bring him a Bible, as he didn't own one. We worked slightly different shifts, so I wouldn't be able to pass off the Bible in the parking garage, and I was not comfortable doing so within the building. I told him I simply couldn't do it, as that would be against company policy. I had been warned after all. He begged and pleaded. Then he told me that a friend of his always left him the morning paper, once he'd finished reading it, on his desk. He suggested that I could place the Bible on his desk, under the newspaper, where he would retrieve it when he came in. This way no one would ever have to know. I finally agreed. He hugged me, thanked me and went back to work.

The following day I did as he had asked me. I even wrote him a short note of encouragement inside the cover. Toward the end of the day I was called to the human resources office where the newspaper, the Bible, and the young man were all present. I looked at him, he turned toward me and grinned, and I shook my head. I was let go. Rumors ran wild. I had supposedly been caught lying to customers, cheating, etc.

I was not there to defend myself, and no one stood up for my character, because several in management had been working together to take me down. If any had come forward to testify of my good character, they would have to admit the deceitful way they had played on my heart with this young man who was supposedly seeking godly advice.

Obviously the organization was willing to forego a certain amount of honest profit in order to persecute me and remove me from their company. I was, and had been, an excellent worker, winning a plethora of sales awards. And I had certainly made them lots of money.

But, my own foolishness was at play here too. I should have been wiser. I discovered, though, that I was strong enough in Him to survive this experience. After all there are those in foreign countries who are tortured and killed for following Jesus. My minor persecution was nothing compared to the hell they endure. I hoped the young man would think about the things we had discussed. And, when I felt anxious about losing my job, as I went in search of another, I remembered this scripture, and it comforted me:

"Let your reasonableness be known to everyone. The Lord is at hand, do not be anxious about anything, but in everything by prayer and supplication with thanksgiving let your requests be known to God. And the peace of God, which surpasses all understanding, will guard your hearts and your minds in Christ Jesus. Finally, brothers, whatever is true, whatever is honorable, whatever is just, whatever is pure, whatever is lovely, whatever is commendable, if there is any excellence, if there is anything worthy of praise, think about these things. What you have learned and received and heard and seen in me-practice these things, and the God of peace will be with you." Philippians 4:5-9

And, of course God was faithful. He kept my heart at peace, but He also quickly supplied another job. This time as the office manager of a large church, where my penchant for sharing the Gospel would not be so frowned upon. I worked there until my stage 4 cancer diagnosis in October of 2010, when I would be forced to spend so much time at the cancer center, that I simply couldn't continue my work at the church. God is good, and He always supplied our needs.

"And my God will supply every need of yours according to His riches in glory in Christ Jesus." Philippians 4:19

I know now that I can trust the Lord for the big things, and for the little things. He cares about it all. He will never leave us or forsake us. Tell everyone who is insecure, helpless, hopeless, or filled with self hatred not to be discouraged. Reach out to God and He will run to your rescue.

"The Lord will rescue me from every evil deed and bring me safely into His heavenly kingdom. To Him be the glory forever and ever. Amen." 2 Timothy 4:19

I have said these things to you, that in Me you may have peace. In the world you will have tribulation. But take heart; I have overcome the world.

> John 16:33

SATAN'S MANY NAMES —ANXIETY AND STRESS

As a little girl I worried all the time and continually looked over my shoulder expecting monsters to attack. I had to be on constant watch for those who would do me and my siblings, harm. After all, I had a duty to protect them; first from our father, later from all the men in our mom's life and finally when her drinking was at its worse, from her. I was a light sleeper and woke often in the midst of terrible nightmares.

By the age of ten and a half I'd learned to prop a chair under the door handle of our bedroom to keep out unwanted visitors and listened intently, day and night, for the second shoe to drop. With adults around me who went ballistic at the smallest things, I had to be ever ready to duck and hide. All this worry and stress culminated in bleeding ulcers by the time I was eleven years old. This continued into my adulthood. Because, even when I wasn't a child anymore, I was still surrounded by people who would do me harm. I'm still jumpy, even though I no longer feel afraid all the time. I guess some habits are harder to break than others.

I adopted a saying during those years. One that I said with a chuckle, but meant very seriously. It was a stupid saying. But, as I've told you before, I've done and said lots of stupid things, and I'm usually the first person to tell on myself when I discover the error. When folks would ask me if I was a worrier, I would tell them. "Well, I might as well worry, I'm good at it. It's probably the one thing I do better than God." Now, tell me, after your read that, why I wasn't struck by lightning one stormy day? What a dumb thing to say, huh?

Now I know that worry is very unproductive. I know that 99% of the things we worry about never happen. I know by worrying we shave years off of our own life expectancy. And I know that when we worry, we are admitting we don't trust God enough to take care of it for us. Worry is a waste of time and energy. I know that now. I didn't know that then.

The latest CDC report states that over One hundred and ten million, that is 110,000,000 people die every year as a direct result of stress. Seven (7) people every two (2) seconds! Back in those days I didn't know that the fear, pounding heart rate, rapid breathing, tense muscles and anxiety were signs of stress, or how to deal with it. Who knew that it could contribute to some of the leading causes of death in Americans, such as: Heart Disease; High blood pressure; Diabetes; Depression; and Anxiety disorder, among others. I sure didn't. I do now.

Jesus spoke about this very thing in Luke 21:25 and 26. It says, *"And there will be signs in sun and moon and stars and on the earth distress of nations in perplexity because of the roaring of the sea and the waves, people fainting with fear and with foreboding of what is coming on the world. For the powers of the heavens will be shaken."*

I can just see Satan sitting on his black throne in hell, clapping his hands and laughing gleefully each time one of us allows stress to take us down. We need to get a handle on this! Medical sites will give you all sorts of ideas and methods, including drugs, to overcome stress and anxiety. But, I'm here to tell you that there is no better answer to controlling stress than prayer. Discovering this over these past years, since my cancer diagnosis in 2010, has quite literally saved my life. Now, when I am in doubt; when I feel upset or anxious; when my heart begins to pound; my pulse quickens; my muscles tense, or I catch myself breathing rapidly; I stop whatever I'm doing, or saying and pray. Don't ever stop praying. Prayer is powerful. God hears prayer and God answers prayer.

One of my biggest lessons over the past few years has been not to worry about what will happen tomorrow. We are not promised a tomorrow, so tomorrow is a gift. Don't make it a gift you don't want to open.

"Therefore do not be anxious about tomorrow, for tomorrow will be anxious for itself. Sufficient for the day is its own trouble." Matthew 6:34

Knowing there is a God in heaven who really cares about me has been a blessing. Trusting what His Word says was tough at first, but has gotten easier over time. He has proved Himself to me in so many ways and through so many miracles that I would be a fool to doubt him now. I have also been blessed to be, in some cases, the hands He has used to perform a miracle for someone else.

An example of that would be: I had a pastor friend a while back who led a very large congregation. He and I were having a discussion one day and he admitted to me that he wasn't sure Jesus had ever really lived.

He was pretty sure that perhaps, instead of an actual person hanging on the cross, it was a spectral image. I told him, since he seemed unaware that Gnostics during the years following the death, burial and resurrection of Jesus, held some of the same false beliefs. They considered themselves to have a superior knowledge even than what is contained in the Word of God.

I told him the Bible speaks of and condemns that thinking. Then he commented that just because something is in the Bible, doesn't mean it is true. Well, I happen to believe that is exactly what it means. By now I was standing with my mouth agape. It was hard for me to believe this man was ministering in a church, but didn't seem to really believe in God. Why would he even want to represent a God he didn't believe in? I prayed for a way to help him see.

A couple of months later I got a call. This pastor had been diagnosed with brain tumors. When I went to visit he told me that the scans showed the tumors had grown long tendrils which were wrapped in and throughout his brain like dandelion roots. There would be an upcoming surgery, but the surgeon doing the procedure wasn't very hopeful.

He thought he might be able to remove the main tumors in their entirety, but those tendrils were unreachable, and would ultimately sprout new growths. So, it was just a matter of months. The surgeon was hoping to give the pastor a little more time with his family, before the cancer overtook his brain entirely.

I offered to lay hands on him and pray for healing, but he was unimpressed. He laughingly told me he didn't believe in all that 'mumbo jumbo'. I left and continued to pray for guidance, and a way to help him see that there is a 'real' God who loves him and wants to heal him. God is so good, and, not surprisingly, He answered my prayer.

The day before his surgery I got a desperate call. He wanted me to come see him. When I walked into his office he looked at me, bent forward, and patted himself on the top of his head, indicating that he wanted me to pray for him.

I prayed for peace, and for heavenly guidance for the surgeon's hands. Then I claimed the healing that is already promised to us by God's Word, and by His sacrifice on the cross. Using these words from *1 Peter 2:21-25 "For to this you have been called, because Christ also suffered for you, leaving you an example, so that you might follow in His steps. He committed no sin, neither was deceit found in His mouth. When He was reviled, He did not revile in return; when He suffered, He did not threaten, but continued entrusting Himself to Him who judges justly. He Himself bore our sins in His body on the tree, that we might die to sin and live to righteousness. BY HIS WOUNDS YOU HAVE BEEN HEALED. For you were straying like sheep, but have now returned to the Shepherd and Overseer of your souls."*

What a powerful piece of scripture! It just gives me chills every time I read it. And, to say it out loud is a mighty reminder. The next day this pastor had surgery. When he was wheeled out, I got a call from his wife. She was in tears. It seemed that somehow; the doctor called it a miracle; when the surgeon opened his skull, expecting to do a little digging to try and remove as much of the twisting and traveling tendrils as possible; what he found left him with his mouth hanging open. The tumors were sitting, ever so perfectly, on top of his brain. And, all the tendrils that had formerly been entangled and winding throughout the brain were wrapped, very neatly, around the tumors, like tidy little packages. He had only to pluck them out of the cranial cavity, and close the skull.

That pastor never claimed again that he didn't believe Jesus was real. What a mighty God we serve!

Once I came to know the Lord more intimately, I still had a hard time completely opening up. There were times when I felt I shouldn't burden God with all of my ridiculous little worries and cares. Certainly He has better things to do than listen to my problems. I mean, I can see if it is a big thing, you know, some major life event or emergency, but the tiny things? No, I clammed up and refused to pray about what I considered to be the insignificant little messes. That is, until I did a little more reading. God doesn't only want us to come to Him when there is an emergency. He wants us to be in constant contact. Praying without ceasing.

That actually sounds much harder than it is. Once you are in a relationship with the Lord that relies entirely on Him, prayer is no longer your second thought, but indeed, second nature. The Greek word used in 1 Thessalonians 5:17 for "without ceasing" is adialeiptos. The meaning of the word is closer to, 'constantly recurring' than 'nonstop'. So, god doesn't mean you should be on your knees twenty four hours a day. He means He wants to be our first 'go to', instead of our 'last resort'. I find myself having conversations with the Father all day long, and I know that is the cause of my peace.

"Humble yourselves, therefore, under the mighty hand of God so that at the proper time He may exalt you, casting all your anxieties on Him, because He cares for you." 1 Peter 5:6,7

"I sought the Lord, and He answered me and delivered me from all my fears." Psalm 34:4

"Rejoice always, pray without ceasing, give thanks in all circumstances; for this is the will of God in Christ Jesus for you." 1 Thessalonians 5:16,17

There are those who curse their fathers and do not bless their mothers. There are those who are clean in their own eyes but are not washed of their filth. There are those - how lofty are their eyes, how high their eyelids lift! There are those whose teeth are swords, whose fangs are knives, to devour the poor from off the earth, the needy from among mankind.

Proverbs 30:11-14

SATAN'S MANY NAMES —SELF RIGHTEOUSNESS

Self Righteousness. This is a good one, and I'm sure one of Satan's favorites. It's the one where we get to pretend we are better than others, because we are so religious. God can't possibly have a problem with us being religious can He? Well, yes, He certainly can. Jesus didn't die so we could join a religion. He came to set us free from all the pomp and circumstance of fake religiosity. To teach us how to love others, and ourselves, the way He loves.

I can tell you, from personal experience, all about living in a state of self righteousness. You know, I spent so many years feeling as if God had completely abandoned me, that I just figured he didn't care. He certainly hadn't heard my cries for help, as a child, had He? Or, if He had, it seemed He'd ignored them. I got so used to going it on my own that I didn't think I needed Him in order to be okay. I was doing just fine. Well, of course I really wasn't; but I would never have admitted that to anyone. I was a strong woman after all.

Then I met and married Pastor Marty. Poor guy. He got way more than he bargained for on that one. I entered our marriage with more baggage than the contents of the cargo hold of a 747. At the point in time when I met Marty I had never read a Bible in my life. I was considered intelligent and had read thousands of other books, just not the Bible. Oh, I'd been to church a few times with Pastor and Mrs. Brown, (I talked about them a bit in 'When All Else Fails') when I was a little girl; but it certainly wasn't a regular thing, and hadn't happened much at all in recent memory.

So, here I was married to a pastor. I wasn't prepared for that in any way, shape or form. As a matter of fact, for anyone who knew my story and background, I would have been the last person in the world who should have been 'The Pastor's Wife'. However, as I said before, I have read thousands of books. I am a very fast reader and a quick study. I could fake my way through almost any situation when I needed to. I read through the Bible four times in the first year of our marriage, as well as a stack of other 'religious' resources. Once we accepted a 'call' from a larger church, I studied for a license in the denomination for which my husband was currently serving and was hired by the congregation as Marty's associate pastor. I felt prepared to take on the world!

Now, I'm not going to say I was a complete fake. I truly loved the people in our congregation and our church families over the years. I grew close to them and cared deeply for them and their various issues. I held babies, helped decorate for weddings and cried at funerals. I made soup and visited the sick, hung out in hospital rooms at all times of the night and day with families of the sick and dying, visited those in jails and prisons and spent time with Marty visiting shut-ins at their homes and in nursing facilities.

I wrote cards to those members who sprang to mind throughout the week, only to find out later that they were in the midst of a crisis and the card encouraged them at the precise moment they needed it most. I taught Sunday school and VBS, and I worked hard to put on special family nights, holiday programs and community events. All, (as every pastor's wife knows), while taking care of my own family, a house and yard, and even working a full time job outside the church.

The real issue was that I could barely control my own life or thoughts. And though I think I covered fairly well, I was forever scrambling. How could I possibly be responsible for directing the paths of others? When I prayed I was quite eloquent, as I've always had a way with words. People came to me after services with words of praise about my 'heartfelt' prayers. Heartfelt? I don't know about that. When I read the Bible

I understood, intellectually, the words I was reading. My problem was that those words resonating in my mind, didn't make it as far as my heart. There was no life in the words I prayed. They were just flowery babble.

None of the phony baloney stuff was intentional. I wasn't trying to scam anyone. I just didn't know how to connect with God and I was too ashamed to admit it. I was the pastor's wife for crying out loud so I should know this stuff right? How could I truly be a representative of the Lord and be teaching others, when I just knew in my heart He didn't really care about me?

Then there was a series of events that started me thinking. First my daughter was cured of a grave illness. Marty was healed of a condition that had afflicted him for decades. My hearing was restored (my eardrums had ruptured when I was a child and I had been hard of hearing most of my life). We were seeing some pretty remarkable miracles happening all around us. I wondered if perhaps I had been too hard on God? And then I thought, "No", it wasn't as if I hadn't believed there was a God. I had always been pretty sure He existed. I just didn't think He had time for me. Could I be wrong?

Throughout it all, as my intellectual biblical knowledge grew, I felt responsible to be sure that our children, and all of our church family members, knew what rules they should be following in order to please God. I think it started out innocently enough. Just wanting them to be in God's will. Just wanting them to be safe, and assured of God's mercy. I mean, I wasn't absolutely certain about myself yet, but I was pretty sure if I worked hard enough at it I would be assured a place in heaven. I wanted them to be there too. I just needed to work harder, that's all; and make sure all those who'd been placed in our care did as well.

When your biblical knowledge only goes as far as your head, and doesn't make it all the way to your heart, this is where the biggest problems start. And what began innocently enough: wanting to be a good pastor's wife; wanting to do the right thing for the people in our care; and just wanting to do the right thing for once in my life, soon became a problem. I was sure it was my responsibility to be sure each and every one of these people made it to heaven. Not just to introduce them to the Savior, mind you, but to make sure they were following every single commandment to the letter.

By now I had read the Bible over and over, multiple times, so I knew all the 'rules' inside and out. I began to feel like I had all 'the answers'; that perhaps I really was supposed to be right where I was, for such a time as this, (and all that really important spiritual sounding stuff). That the salvation of the world just might possibly be resting on my shoulders. My demeanor changed. I turned in to that 'religious' leader, with the iron fist, who is sure they have it all down to the letter. The religious leader you want to avoid at all costs.

Yes, I am deeply ashamed to say I was that self-righteous leader, the one who eventually thought she knew it all and may even have put other's eternal lives in jeopardy by my arrogance. Only now, through my books, speaking engagements and further contact, do I have an opportunity to correct that haughty and misguided interpretation of salvation I held through my own self-righteousness.

I have since talked to many of the people in those early congregations and they tell me I judge myself too harshly. I don't know. They tell me they always felt loved by Marty and I. But I know now that what I was teaching them, without really being aware of my error at the time, was that they could somehow work in order to earn a place in heaven by keeping the laws. Now I know that only the Grace of God, through the love and sacrifice of Jesus Christ, can pay that debt for us.

"For by grace you have been saved through faith. And this is not your own doing; it is the gift of God,

not the result of works, so that no one may boast." Ephesians 2:8,9

As much as it might have seemed, as I looked back on that time, I guess I didn't have the market on self-righteousness cornered. There seems to be plenty to go around and always has been. When I was a girl, living in upper state New York, I boarded a bus one Sunday morning, with my younger siblings, to attend a Christian church youth service in town. We arrived and the younger children were taken to classes appropriate for their age group. We were new in the area and I was relieved to see a couple of kids from my new school in my group. Kids who immediately proceeded to ignore me and giggle behind my back.

The young minister preached for an hour or

so and then invited us to come forward to accept Christ as Savior. I had asked Jesus into my life in Pastor Brown's church, at nine years old and, I might add, every night since then for years. And though I never really felt 'saved', as I continued to make mistakes every day, this fellow made me feel a little uncomfortable as he continued with his invitation to come to Jesus. All the while looking directly at me. After services, we left for the day and went home. The children and I decided not to attend the following day's youth service. The next evening there was a knock on the trailer door where we lived and when I opened it that same young pastor was standing on the step.

He proceeded to tell me that God had directed him to come to me and 'save' me. I told him he was making me uncomfortable. I asked him to leave. He got angry and yelled, "Why won't you let me save you? I'm here to save you. Are you stupid girl?" I showed him the door, and never went back to that youth gathering. I didn't quite understand his wording, at the church, or on my doorstep. It sure sounded to me as though he thought he would be the one doing the saving and not Jesus, so my gut told me to run in the other direction. That felt to me like the epitome of self-righteousness. And I absolutely knew he thought himself better than I. The funny thing about that encounter was that I had never felt 'good enough' in my entire life, but this man making me feel 'less than' caused something to rise up in me. I would work for decades trying to make others like me and believe I was worthy.

I have since met other ministers and religious

leaders who are involved in deliverance or healing ministries. Most of us are aware that it is Jesus doing the healing, and that He can use any hands He wants to serve His purpose. Because, after all, the healing is not coming from the minister's hands, but from the true source, the Father.

However, some get caught up in the excitement. Perhaps innocently enough to start. And begin to believe that they are that source of healing not merely the conduit. God will not allow us to steal His glory for any extended length of time, before He steps in and puts all things right. It is bad enough to assume you are worthy of God's Grace by your own merit; but another whole level of self-righteousness, to think you are the source of His Grace or healing.

"But when the goodness and loving kindness of

God our Savior appeared, He saved us, not because of works done by us in righteousness, but according to His own mercy by the washing of regeneration and renewal of the Holy Spirit, whom He poured out on us richly through Jesus Christ our Savior, so that being justified by His grace we might become heirs According to the hope of eternal life." Titus 3:4-7

I am eternally grateful to my Father. That He allowed me to experience some very scary things which caused me to seek the Truth more earnestly. I'm also grateful to know that my salvation is not contingent upon me in any way, other than that I accept His freely given gift of Grace. That no number of good acts will earn me His love, but no amount of mistakes will take His love away either. I am grateful because, I became so weary of trying to earn something that cannot be earned; trying to win something that has already been won; and coming up short on my own each and every time. Now that I know this is a gift that can't be earned by my own effort, I am free to share it with whomever I wish, because they don't have to earn it either.

"Listen to Me, you stubborn of heart, you who are far from righteousness; I bring near My righteousness; it is not far off, and my salvation will not delay; I will put salvation in Zion, for Israel My glory." Isaiah 46:12,13

I am a firm believer that if we become too full of ourselves and allow feelings of self-righteousness to control our actions, He cannot, and indeed will not, fill us with His goodness. Until I finally let go of the wrong assumption that I could do anything aside from His Grace, I was dead in the water. Now, I lean on Him, fully aware that I can absolutely do nothing of myself. What a relief to serve an able and willing Savior!!

"As it is written: "None is righteous, no, not one." Romans 3:10

May we, each one of us, remember that Jesus died to save us from our sin. He was sinless, yet He gave Himself for us. He didn't deserve the death He died. But He suffered that humiliation, and horror, so we wouldn't have to.

"Surely He has borne our griefs and carried our sorrows; yet we esteemed Him stricken, smitten by God, and afflicted. But He was wounded for our transgressions; He was crushed for our iniquities; upon Him was the chastisement that brought us peace, and with His stripes we are healed. All we

like sheep have gone astray; we have turned - every one - to his own way; and the Lord has laid on Him the iniquity of us all." Isaiah 53:4-6

I will be eternally grateful for the stripes He took, the scars He wears, and the suffering He endured for me. And, I know that because of His Love, I am free.

Therefore the kingdom of heaven may be compared to a king who wished to settle accounts with his servants. When he began to settle, one was brought to him who owed him ten thousand talents. And since he could not pay, his master ordered him to be sold, with his wife and children and all that he had, and payment to be made. So the servant fell on his knees, imploring him, "Have patience with me, and I will pay you everything". And out of pity for him, the master of that servant released him and forgave him the debt. But when that same servant went out, he found one of his fellow servants who owed him a hundred denarii, and seizing him, he began to choke him, saying, "Pay what you owe." So his fellow servant fell down and pleaded with him, "Have patience with me, and I will pay you." He refused and went and put him in prison until he should pay the debt. When his fellow servants saw what had taken place, they were greatly distressed, and they went and reported to their master all that had taken place. Then his master summoned him and said to him, "You wicked servant! I forgave you all that debt because you pleaded with me. And should not you have had mercy on your fellow servant, as I had mercy on you?" And in anger his master delivered him to the jailers, until he should pay all his debt. "So also my heavenly Father will do to every one of you, if you do not forgive your brother from your heart.

Matthew 18:23-35

SATAN'S MANY NAMES —UN-FORGIVENESS

I've heard every excuse in the book for why someone shouldn't be expected to forgive, including a few I made up myself. "Pastor, you just have no idea what this person did to me. How could God ever expect me to forgive them?" Oh, I don't know? Why don't we ask Jesus, for starters. He who hung on a cross to pay for our debts, so we could have forgiveness from the Father without deserving it, and without paying for it. I'll bet he would see whatever 'horrible' transgression we can't seem to get past, or let go of, as pretty mild compared to the crown of thorns beat into His skull, the flesh ripping lashing he took and the nails which were pounded into his feet and wrists. I'm pretty sure hanging on a cross is more than most of us have ever experienced, certainly more than I have ever endured. And yet, the Son of God had only forgiveness on His mind, *"And Jesus said, 'Father, forgive them, for they know not what they do.' And they cast lots to divide His garments." Luke 23:34*

I spent decades wallowing in self pity and un-forgiveness. How could I think of forgiving my father after the things he did to me? And the men my mother brought home? The shame I carried for so long due to their sexual abuse. Shouldn't they all have to pay? However, the longer I carried that hatred and un-forgiveness, the more I was torn apart inside. Bleeding ulcers, migraine headaches, sleepless nights, all ailments which started when I was a girl. The people who hurt me weren't suffering as I lay awake at night despising them. It was only me. I was dying from the inside out.

I discovered that forgiveness wasn't about letting others off the hook. It was about allowing myself to heal, starting immediately. I am a happier person now. I feel physically better when I am not filled to the brim with the venom of un-forgiveness.

Un-forgiveness hinders our faith. The Father won't forgive our sins, if we refuse to forgive others. After all, you know, we reap what we sow. Sow mercy to reap mercy, sow judgment to reap judgment. Believe me, living an angry, judgmental, and un-forgiving life is a painful and unproductive way to live.

Yes, forgiveness can be difficult. We tend to judge another's right to be forgiven by our own level of hurt. If you hurt me a little, I might consider forgiveness, under the right circumstances; but if you hurt me a lot, forget it! And of course everyone's estimation of 'a lot' is different. But God doesn't want us to weigh in with our own opinions on this matter. He has already told us, in no uncertain terms, to forgive. We are to forgive, as He has forgiven us. So, by laying our anger and hurt at the foot of the cross, we are obeying Him and His direct admonition for us to love one another, no matter what.

That obedience is like a seed. And as hard as it might be to plant the first seed, to let it go once and for all; after that first seed of obedience is sown, He will cause it to grow into full fledged forgiveness. A forgiveness that might actually serve as a witness to someone else. Perhaps even the person who has hurt us. That witness coming to know God's forgiveness, may result in another soul for the kingdom.

Then, what if others who have had a difficult time forgiving, see us forgiving another who has done us a terrible wrong? What if our act of obedience causes someone to question their own stubbornness? What if they decide that if we can forgive the appalling thing which was done to us, surely they can do the same? What if that example of love lights a fire under them and they reach out to forgive as well? We might start an avalanche of forgiveness. One that brings many others to the love and light of the Gospel. Let that light so shine through you.

If you would truly like to flourish in your walk with the Lord, learn to do the difficult things, with His help of course. I have heard far too many people tell me; whether about forgiveness or other necessary tasks; "It's too 'hard'". Well, God will give us the strength, the tools, and the favor to do everything He has set before us, even the 'hard' stuff. We were created for the 'hard' stuff. He never expects us to do things that cannot be done. He expects us to do those things which were assigned to us from the beginning of our life with Him. And then, only with His help. Forgiveness is one of those things.

"And Jesus answered them, "Have faith in God. Truly I say to you, whoever says to this mountain, 'Be taken up and thrown in to the sea,' and does not

doubt in his heart, but believes that what he says will come to pass, it will be done for him. Therefore I tell you, whatever you ask in prayer, believe that you have received it, and it will be yours. And whenever you stand praying, forgive, if you have anything against anyone, so that your Father also who is in heaven may forgive you your trespasses." Mark 11:22-25

Another very good reason to forgive? Forgiveness keeps Satan from getting an advantage over us. That old devil is always looking for ways to gain a foothold in our lives. The minute he gains a foothold; the anger and hatred that accompanies un-forgiveness; he can grow that into a stronghold. We are meant, with help from the Lord, to pull down strongholds not help to build them. So, be quick to forgive. Don't allow

Satan to torture you and drag you down.

"Anyone whom you forgive, I also forgive. Indeed, what I have forgiven, if I have forgiven anything, has been for your sake in the presence of Christ, so that we would not be outwitted by Satan; for we are not ignorant of his designs." 2 Corinthians 2:10,11

As I said before, it can be difficult to forgive. But, it doesn't just happen. I have found that I have to make a conscious decision to forgive. Often I forgive when the person who wronged me has not even apologized. But, remember, I am not forgiving for them. I am forgiving for me. I can't just hang around and wait till I 'feel' like it, or it will never happen. I don't know about you, but I'm not that nice. When I determine that I am going to do the right thing, simply because that is what God has told me to do, my wounded emotions eventually follow, and Satan doesn't have the opportunity to fill my head with so many bitter thoughts.

As I have grown in my walk, I have found it a little easier to forgive. I have also discovered that the quicker I forgive, the less it stings. Forgive quickly, and forgive often.

But, wait a minute. How often should I forgive? What if I have a friend or relative who continually messes up? Should I forgive them over and over? Doesn't that just encourage the same rotten behavior? This is one I have struggled with for years. We all have that person, or persons, who continue to hurt us. No matter how many times we have helped them, lent them money, got them out of trouble, or forgiven a personal affront. And continual forgiveness just seems to beg for additional mistreatment from them, doesn't it?

God doesn't ask us to continue putting ourselves back in the position where we were hurt. And He isn't saying that what the other person did to you is okay. Forgiveness isn't permission for the other to continue abusing you. Forgiveness is just that, forgiveness. Now, if that person is hurting you over and over, remove yourself from the abusive situation. Permanently if necessary. But, if they ask you for forgiveness, grant their request. Remember that un-forgiveness hurts you much more than it hurts the other person.

"Pay attention to yourselves! If your brother sins, rebuke him, and if he repents, forgive him, and if he sins against you seven times in the day, and turns to you seven times, saying, 'I repent', you must forgive

him." Luke 17:3,4

"Then Peter came up and said to him, 'Lord, how often will my brother sin against me, and I forgive him?' Jesus said to him, 'I do not say to you seven times, but seventy times seven.'" Matthew 18:21,22

Who should we forgive? Forgive everyone. *"Freely you have received, freely give."* What if the offence was too grievous? We have all sinned. And, in God's eyes there is no sin better or worse than any other. Sin is sin.

And, forgive God, if you are angry with Him. If your life didn't turn out the way you thought it should. If there was pain in your childhood that left you wondering, why? The death of a loved one. Situations that seemed unfair. God is always just. There might be things you don't understand now, but God loves you!

People often make a huge mistake when they shut God out of their lives after a personal tragedy and refuse to receive help from the only one in the universe who can actually help them! Jesus died for all people, for all time, for all sin. When He rose again from the grave, He gave each and every one of us a way out of our sin and a bridge to eternity with the Father. By confessing that He is the Son of God, that He died for my sins and rose again to overcome death, and by asking Him to come into my heart to be my Savior and Lord, I accept that free gift of Grace available to everyone.

Now, here is the really hard part. You have forgiven, so stop talking about it. Quit telling all your friends and everyone you run into about the circumstances that made you angry. Quit gossiping behind the back of the person you've already forgiven. To continue talking about it just stirs up old feelings and results in bursts of renewed anger. Once you have forgiven, let it go. That doesn't mean allow it to happen again, if you are able to change your situation. But, go on with your life. If possible, so far as it depends on you, live peaceably with all.

"Bless those who persecute you; bless and do not curse them. Rejoice with those who rejoice, weep with those who weep. Live in harmony with one another. Do not be haughty, but associate with the lowly. Never be wise in your own sight. Repay no one evil for evil, but give thought to what is honorable in the sight of all. If possible, so far as it depends on you, live peaceably with all. Beloved, never avenge

yourselves, but leave it to the wrath of God, for it is written, "Vengeance is mine, I will repay, says the Lord." Romans 12:14-19

"In Him we have redemption through His blood, the forgiveness of our trespasses, according to the riches of His grace." Ephesians 1:7

"Be angry and do not sin; do not let the sun go down on your anger, and give no opportunity to the devil." Ephesians 4:6,7

In this day and age, with political correctness run amuck and our nation divided between left and right. Liberals and conservatives fighting to be heard and screaming to be hailed 'right', there are lots of hurt feelings. As Christians, we have a constitutional right to express our views and opinions, just as the rest of the world does. However, let us not be the ones who use foul language, name calling, and angry taunts in our discourse. If we do not agree, then we can agree to disagree. If someone becomes angry, be quick to make amends, forgiving often. Let us be the voice of reason in a bitter and broken nation.

The thief comes only to steal and kill and destroy. I came that they may have life and have it abundantly.

                                John 10:10

OPENING OUR EYES

What a wonderful piece of scripture to help us transition from darkness to light. Notice in the scripture, which begins this chapter; Satan is Fear and destruction, but Jesus is abundant life. This would be the perfect place to uncover a little about who Satan really is, but more importantly, to begin to uncover the truth of who God really is, especially who He is to those who love and trust in Him.

We have just covered multiple names of the enemy, but aside from those names we've examined, we must be aware of his intent; his incessant, eternal, evil intent.

If you are child of the most High God; if

you are born again; if you trust in Jesus, Satan hates you. It's pretty simple. This might sound harsh, but it is very true. In your current state, he knows he can't have you because you belong to the Savior, but he will do anything and everything in his power to trip you up, and to keep you from sharing the Gospel with others. How many 'Christians' do you know who do not share their faith? Or, perhaps I should ask how many Christians you know who DO share the Gospel with others? I'm sure the list, sadly, would be much shorter. Have you ever wondered why? Again, the answer is Satan.

Do you remember the parable of the seed and the sower which appears in all three of the synoptic Gospels? Matthew 13:1-23, Mark 4:1-20 and Luke 8:4-15. Go to Matthew 13:1-

9 and read, then take in Jesus' explanation of that parable (below) to His disciples. *"When anyone hears the Word of the Kingdom and does not understand it, the evil one (Satan) comes and snatches away what has been sown in his heart. This is what was sown along the path. As for what was sown on rocky ground, this is the one who hears the word and immediately receives it with joy, yet he has no root in himself, but endures for a while, and when tribulation or persecution arises on account of the Word, immediately he falls away. As for what was sown among thorns, this is the one who hears the Word, but the cares of the world and the deceitfulness of riches choke the Word, and it proves unfruitful. As for what was sown on good soil, this is the one who hears the Word and understands it. He indeed bears fruit and yields, in one case*

a hundredfold, in another sixty, and in another thirty." Matthew 13:19-23

Let's see. The first example. An individual who hears the Word of the Kingdom, but doesn't understand. So, Satan comes along and snatches away what was planted in his heart. This is one of the very reasons why it is so important for us to not only share the Gospel, but to make disciples. When we introduce a new believer to Jesus, helping them to find a Bible believing church, and additional study opportunities, is imperative to their further growth and the further assurance that they will not fall away. Well, why should I do that? Isn't that the pastor's job? Dear loved ones in Christ, We are all commanded to "Go ye into all the world, preaching the Gospel to every creature." I don't want to see anyone damned to hell, do you? Then do all you can to see those who are new to the faith, find all the help they need to thrive in Christ.

The next category is the seed which falls on rocky ground. He receives it with joy, but has no root in himself. He endures for a while, but hard times or ridicule because of the Word causes him to fall away. We can't see the condition of another's heart, so this one is a bit trickier. Many people will face ridicule, hard times and persecution due to their new faith in Christ. In many places around the world, even death.

If they asked Jesus to be their Savior, in the heat of the moment, but have no real intention of making Him Lord of their life, then they might well allow others to pull them away. As believers, we can encourage new believers, invite them to attend services with us, and be there to offer godly advice. However, the final decision as to what they will do with their eternity is up to them.

And then there are the thorns. Seed is sown, but falls among the thorns where the cares of the world and deceitfulness of riches chokes out the Word. What does that mean? Something bad happens and we blame God, or wonder why He didn't protect us. I mean, now that I'm a Christian nothing bad is ever supposed to happen to me again, right? No, my friend, that is when Satan's attacks arise anew. It was one thing when he was trying to keep you from becoming a Christian. That was bad enough in his eyes. But now that you are excited and trying to share the 'Good News' with others, he is going to get really mad and stomp down hard!

I am not trying to scare you. You must remember that, as a child of the most high King, you are always in His mighty and powerful hands. However, be prepared to stand strong and get ready for the attacks of the enemy.

And, the riches? Well sometimes, once we are saved, the Lord asks us to sacrifice something. Don't worry, it's only stuff. But, that can be a tough one for those of us who have perhaps put too much stock in material things. It isn't that God doesn't want us to have stuff; it's more that He doesn't want stuff to have us. Remember the rich young man?

"And as He was setting out on His journey, a man ran up and knelt before Him and asked Him, "Good Teacher, what must I do to inherit eternal

life?" And Jesus said to him, "Why do you call Me good? No one is good except God alone. You know the commandments: Do not murder, Do not commit adultery, Do not steal, Do not bear false witness, Do not defraud, Honor your father and mother." And he said to Him, "Teacher, all these I have kept from my youth." And Jesus, looking at him, loved him, and said to him, "You lack one thing: go, sell all that you have and give to the poor, and you will have treasure in heaven; and come follow Me." Disheartened by the saying, he went away sorrowful, for he had great possessions." Mark 10:17-22

As Christians we are often quick to boast, "I would give up everything for Jesus", but I have to let you know, when you say that to God, He will tell you He doesn't want everything, He wants that one little thing you've held back. You know, the very small thing that you didn't think He'd really notice, or want, anyway. The tiny thing you carry in a secret place.

Jesus is pretty smart. He is God after all. Every situation that can befall a new Christian, and cause him to fall away from his new faith, is listed in the explanation of His parable of the sower and the seed.

Why is it then, that when some people hear the greatest news of all time, they don't head out to shout it from the rooftops? Satan, that's why. Are you one that never really understood the Gospel message? But instead of studying the Word to discover the whole truth, the simple and beautiful truth, you listened to the world? Perhaps you were very excited about the message of the cross when you first heard it, but then someone you considered to be 'smarter', explained that it couldn't possibly be true. You know all the things the world throws out there: Saying that there are 'discrepancies' in the Bible; or it is just a story passed down from person to person over millennia, so obviously mistakes were made when someone wrote it down. Perhaps someone even told you that other historical records don't back up Biblical accounts?

Those are all lies of Satan.

There are NO actual discrepancies in the Bible. I challenge you to find one. If you think you have, contact me. My website is in the copyright section of this book and all my contact information is on that website.

New Testament Biblical accounts were

actually written within the lifetime of the author involved, including every single one of the Gospel accounts, the book of Acts and all of Paul's writings. And, there are plenty of non-Biblical historical records that back up the Bible. Flavius Josephus, a Jewish historian, who was born shortly after the death and resurrection of Jesus is one source. His twenty volume collection titled, 'Jewish Antiquities' mentions Jesus by name and backs up many Biblical events of the early church. Tacitus, a Roman Historian, yes, a Roman, corroborates many Biblical claims; exactly as they are laid out in the Bible; in, 'Annals of Imperial Rome'.

Archeologists discover new sites every year which prove accounts and persons in the Bible to be true. Josh McDowell wrote a wonderful book entitled "The New Evidence That Demands a Verdict" and he adds updates regularly as more and more proofs are found. This, or a good study Bible with an in depth 'Apologetics' section, will help with some of those pesky questions folks tend to ask when they just don't know, or are perhaps even trying to trip you up. Another good reference source is an online site we use a lot in our ministry: 'answersingenesis.org'.

We are living in exciting, but controversial times. Every lie told by the devil, to try and nullify the Word, can be disproved, if someone is willing to put forth the time and effort to do so. However, there are those who spend their time pulling others away from faith at Satan's evil bidding. And, those who will call you stupid or simple minded for believing in a God who loves;

a God who was willing to sacrifice His only Son to pay for our sins.

Perhaps you have fallen away from faith. Maybe when you were a new Christian terrible things happened in your life. The death of a loved one, financial troubles, an illness. Due to the newness of your faith, and maybe even a false idea about your relationship with the Lord, you blamed God. You see, Our Father God never promised we wouldn't have trouble. He actually told us that He had troubles while He was here in His earthly life. But, He also promised that we would have peace in Him.

"I have said these things to you, that in me you may have peace. In the world you will have tribulation. But take heart, I have overcome the world." John 16:33

Satan wants you to doubt. He counts on it. He wants you to question every scripture in the Bible, without ever actually looking for the truth of it, so that you will think it's all a lie. Because, if he can make you believe there is one lie contained in the text, then why would any of it be true? And, if instead of studying the Word, to show yourself approved, you spend your time doubting and believing his lies, he has won the fight.

The world is a mess. Filled with people who are searching for something. They just don't know what. Satan and his minions work very hard to make certain very few of those newly sown seeds are planted in good soil. He will fill your minds with suspicion, and your life with pain, to try and steal your peace, to turn you away from the one and only Truth who truly matters. But, I promise you, if you will not turn away; if you will trust in the One who sacrificed His life for you, even when it seems too good to be true; you will see the rewards of a Grace filled life in Christ. There is no grander love, no more fulfilling destiny, no life more gratifying, than one spent in the service of and service for Jesus. My heart is full and my being satisfied when I share the Gospel. And when I see someone come to Christ, there is no greater joy.

When Jesus Christ went to the cross, He said (speaking of Satan), *"Now is the prince of this world cast out." John 12:31. Revelation 12:11 says, "And they* (the saints) *overcame him* (Satan) *by the blood of the Lamb and by the word of their testimony."*

Are your sins under the blood of Jesus? Are you saved by His sacrifice?

Satan is a liar. He will destroy you and everyone you know if you give him a chance. Come to know the Lord. And, if you already live in Christ, get to know Him better. The devil cannot deceive you if you hide the Word in your heart. Teach your children, and your grand children, before it is too late. Share the message of Grace with everyone you meet.

Sidlow Baxter once said, "Surely the devil must say to his demons, 'Boys, keep them from prayer! Because if we can keep them from praying, we can beat them every time. But, if they pray, they'll beat us every time.'"

We truly overcome the devil when we who have received Jesus Christ as Lord and Savior take up and put on the Armor of God.

Before any good pilot takes off, he goes

through a checklist, to assure all is well. Our checklist as followers in Christ is listed in the book of Ephesians:

"Finally, be strong in the Lord and in the strength of His might. Put on the whole armor of God, that you may be able to stand against the schemes of the devil. For we do not wrestle against flesh and blood, but against the rulers, against the authorities, against the cosmic powers over this present darkness, against the spiritual forces of evil in the heavenly places. ***Therefore take up the whole armor of God, that you may be able to withstand in the evil day****, and having done all, to stand firm. Stand therefore,* ***having fastened on the belt of truth, and having put on the breastplate of righteousness, and as shoes for your feet, having put on the readiness given by the Gospel of peace****. In all circumstances*

take up the shield of faith, with which you can extinguish all the flaming darts of the evil one; and take the helmet of salvation, and the sword of the Spirit, which is the word of God, praying at all times in the Spirit, with all prayer and supplication. *To that end keep alert with all perseverance, making supplication for all the saints" Ephesians 6:10-18*

Are you saved? Then don't fear. You don't need to flee from the enemy, he will flee from you. You can stand in the Name of Jesus. But if you do not know Jesus, as Savior and Lord, know this. You will not stand apart from Him.

There is no use in praying, "Lord, deliver us from evil," unless you can also pray, "Our Father." Is God your Father? Have you been born again? If God is not your father, then Jesus Christ is not your Savior, and Satan is your master. But, he is a defeated foe. For the Kingdom, the power, and the glory forever belong to God. Do you know Him? Is Jesus Christ real to you? There is no decision you will ever make that will have more impact on your life here and in the hereafter than the decision to follow Christ. Stand therefore.

And He is before all things, and in Him all things hold together.

Colossians 1:17

WHO IS OUR INFINITE GOD?

Now that we are pretty clear on who Satan is and is not; let us concentrate a little more on the Lord. God is completely unlike anything or anyone we could ever know or imagine. He is unique, one of a kind, without comparison. He is holy and perfect. Even trying our very best to describe Him in mere words falls short of capturing who He truly is. Human words simply cannot do justice to our all knowing and wonderful Father.

While completely comprehending who God is remains impossible for us as limited beings,

God does share Himself in a variety of ways, including in His Word and in His creation. Through these things we can begin, if only in the simplest of terms, to wrap our minds around our awesome Creator and God.

Though we may never know all there is to know of the perfect holiness of God; He does possess certain attributes, or characteristics if you will, that we can know, and He's given us His Word, in the Bible, to help us understand Him a bit better.

What are God's attributes? When we speak of God's attributes we are trying to come to terms with who He is, what He is like and what kind of God He is to us.

Some of God's attributes are what theologians call, "incommunicable", which means they are qualities possessed by God alone. Others are, "communicable", which means they are traits which can be possessed by both God and humans, though only He possesses them perfectly.

What follows is a list of some of the attributes of God. I will attempt; in my most imperfect humanity; to show what they mean and why they matter, in hopes that we can come to know His love for us just a little bit better. So, here we go:

GOD IS INFINITE - He is Self-Existing and without origin.

I would have to say that this is one of the hardest attributes for even the staunchest believer to comprehend. He has existed forever, before time as we know it, and has always, just, been. Man did not create God, but God created man. How can that be? How can a being simply exist without being created? Well, simply, He is God. Suffice it to say that it boggles the mind. And, if it confuses you, then you are not alone. Using our limited minds to grasp the nature of a limitless God is like trying to catch the wind in our bare hands. But, in order to give Him credit for creation and complete control of the universe, this is a trait that is necessary.

It takes a great deal of humility to admit there is One who exists outside of all the reasonable human categories we have assigned, who lies beyond our own mortal plane, who has no need to submit to our curious inquiries, and who will not be dismissed with a mere name. More humility than most of us possess, in fact. So, as mere humans, many people try to save face by bringing God down to our own base level, or at least down to a level where we can manage Him more effectively.

Did you know that the name Jehovah is used over 6,800 times in the Bible? In the King James Version of the Bible, it's translated Lord God. The root of this name means "self-existing"; one who never came into being, and one who will always be. The word speaks of His sovereignty, His strength and His goodness. It is the personal covenant name of Israel's God. WOW!

When Moses asked God, "Who shall I tell Pharaoh has sent me?" God said, "I AM THAT I AM." Jehovah, or Yahweh, is the most sacred name in the universe to Jewish scribes. Many will not even pronounce the name out loud.

"Great is our Lord, and abundant in power; His understanding is beyond measure." Psalm 147:5

GOD IS OMNIPOTENT - He is All Powerful

Omnipotent means to have unlimited power (Omni = all; potent = powerful). This means that God is able and powerful and can do anything He wills without any effort on His part. In other words, God is able to do all that He 'desires' to do. When He plans something, it will come to be. If He purposes something, it is bound to happen.

I feel the need to note the "anything He wills" portion of the above comment. Remember that God is good, and cannot do anything that is contrary, or contradictory, to His nature. God's decisions are always in line with His character, and He has all the power to do whatever the heck He decides to do. I have been faced with the flippant question (usually by confused unbelievers), "Can

God create a boulder so big that He can't lift it?" and other equally nonsensical queries. My question back to them is usually, "Why would He ever do that? God has better things to do with His time than fulfill frivolous dares to prove He is God. "

How can we fathom the mysteries of God? Paul tells us that God is *"able to do immeasurably more than all we ask or imagine"*. Although that kind of power seems frightful, remember that God is always good. Though He can do anything, according to His infinite ability, He will only do those things that are consistent with Himself. He cannot lie. He cannot tolerate sin. And He can't save impenitent sinners (those who refuse to repent and put their trust in Jesus).

"By the Word of the Lord the heavens were

made, and by the breath of His mouth all their host." Psalm 33:6

GOD IS OMNISCIENT - He Is All-knowing

God is Omniscient. That means He knows everything. He can be everywhere at the same time. I know, weird concept, huh? However, it is not a weird concept for God. He is God after all. He never sleeps or slumbers. He is aware of every moment of every day and always knows what we're up against. There is no situation or circumstance too small to take to Him. He always knows where we are, so there is no place we can go that He doesn't see us.

I have to say that in the beginning of my walk with the Lord, this one bothered me. Why? Well, I knew that I didn't always act 'company ready', when there was no one around to impress with my good manners. I was, frankly, embarrassed to have God see me at my worst moments. But, that turned out to be a good thing because (and don't get me wrong, I still have plenty of moments I wouldn't want anyone to see); when I know He is always watching, it causes me to check my heart. Perhaps I won't respond so hastily, or maybe I am more compassionate in a certain situation, when I know the Father is watching.

He knows everything in the universe that there ever was to know, everything that is happening right now, and everything that will ever happen. Because God is all-knowing we can trust that He knows everything we are going through today, and everything we will go through in the future. Nothing is too big or too small to take to Him in prayer. This makes it easier to go to Him with everything from the serious to the silly and mundane.

"Remember the former things of old; for I am God, and there is no other; I am God, and there is none like Me, declaring the end from the beginning and from ancient times things not yet done, saying, "My counsel shall stand, and I will accomplish all My purpose," Isaiah 46:9,10

GOD IS OMNIPRESENT - He is Always Everywhere

To be omnipresent means to be in all places, at all times. I know that sounds impossible, but nothing is impossible for God. However, God's being is quite different than the physical matter from which we are made. He, therefore, exists on a plane completely distinguishable from the one which is readily available to the five senses we use.

I find it comforting to know that He is always with us. The fullness of His presence is all around us. This ought to bring great comfort to any Christians who might struggle with deep sorrow or loneliness. In a very real way, God is always near. I don't know about you, but the knowledge that I am never alone gives me a calmness that speaks peace to my soul.

"Where shall I go from Your Spirit? Or where shall I flee from Your presence? If I ascend to heaven, You are there! If I make my bed in Sheol, you are there! If I take the wings of the morning and dwell in the uttermost parts of the sea, even there Your hand shall lead me, and Your right hand shall hold me." Psalm 139:7-10

GOD IS LOVING - God Infinitely and Unchangingly Loves Us Unconditionally

When I first came to Christ, this was one of the hardest concepts for me to accept. The people in my life didn't love this way. To be loved UNCONDITIONALLY was as foreign an idea, as to understand someone taking on the guilt and punishment that should be mine. I was taught to believe that I was the guilty one, all the time and about everything. Many Christians try to tell us that the love of Jesus is so easy that even a little child can understand. But, I am here to tell you that if you are a child or an adult who has never seen love like that, never experienced love like that, it is most certainly NOT a simple idea to comprehend. This is a love that staggers the mind. What a miracle, to be loved this way!

Tozer writes, "It is a strange and beautiful eccentricity of the free God that He has allowed His heart to be emotionally identified with men. Self sufficient as He is, He wants our love and will not be satisfied till He gets it. Free as He is, He has let His heart be bound to us forever. God's love is active, drawing us to Himself. His love is personal. He doesn't love humanity in some vague sense, He loves humans. He loves you and me. And His love for us knows no beginning and no end." Amazing!

"Beloved, let us love one another, for love is from God, and whoever loves has been born of God and knows God. Anyone who does not love does not know God, because God is love." 1John 4:7,8

GOD IS GRACIOUS - God is Infinitely Prone to Spare the Guilty

I should know. I am one of the guilty. The definition of Grace is getting what we don't deserve. In other words, God's love and eternal life with Him.

Tozer (yes I am a huge A.W. Tozer fan, because he was a huge fan of God) wrote, "As mercy is God's goodness confronting human misery and guilt, so grace is His goodness directed toward human debt and demerit. It is by His grace that God imputes merit where none previously existed and declares no debt to be where one had been before."

I am so thankful for God's grace. You know, since grace is a part of who God is, and not just some action He performs, we can trust that His grace is eternal. It isn't something we earn, so it isn't something we can lose by what we say or do.

Praise Him for His infinite grace!

Theologians often differentiate between God's common grace and His saving grace. Christianity Today writer Patrick Mabilog writes this about the difference. "His common grace is a gift to all of mankind. It is the reason that everyone - Christian or non-Christian - enjoys the blessings of life, provision and abundance. Scripture tells us, *"For He makes His sun rise on the evil and on the good, and sends rain on the just and on the unjust." Matthew 5:45*

"While all of humanity benefits from common grace, only those who profess, believe, and put their faith in Christ receive saving grace. This is what results in our sanctification, our justification and our glorification of God, that we might live for Him and enjoy Him for all eternity."

"The Lord is gracious and merciful, slow to anger and abounding in steadfast love. The Lord is good to all, and His mercy is over all that He has made." Psalm 145:8,9

GOD IS MERCIFUL - He is Forever, Unchangeably, Compassionate and Kind

Just as Grace is getting what we don't deserve. Mercy is not getting what we do deserve. God's mercy is inseparable from His justness. Mercy is undeserved, as it should be. After all, deserved mercy would just be another name for justice.

Without the mercy of God, we would have no possible hope of life eternal. Tozer writes, "As judgment is God's justice confronting moral inequity, so mercy is the goodness of God confronting human suffering and guilt. Were there no guilt in the world, no pain and no tears,

God would yet be infinitely merciful; but His mercy might well remain hidden in His heart, unknown to the created universe. No voice would be raised to celebrate the mercy of which none felt the need. It is human misery and sin that call forth the divine mercy."

I know that I am personally, eternally, grateful for the sacrifice of Jesus, and the Grace and Mercy of God. What a mighty God we serve!

"What shall we say then? Is there injustice on God's part? By no means! For He says to Moses, "I will have mercy on whom I have mercy, and I will have compassion on whom I have compassion." Romans 9:14,15

GOD IS JUST - He is Infinitely, Forever Right and Perfect in Everything He Does

So, what is justice? God's justice means more

than that He is simply fair. It means He always does whatever is right and good and reasonable toward everyone. And, though I know this part is hard for many to hear and accept, it also means that when He sentences unrepentant sinners to Hell, it is also right and good.

The natural question which arises from this is, how can a just God justify the unjust? I mean, we are all unjust until we come to Christ, right? We can glean the answer from the Christian doctrine of justification and redemption. Because of the atoning work of Jesus Christ, justice isn't violated when God spares a sinner, but rather satisfied. His mercy does not forbid Him to exercise His justice. And, likewise, His justice does not forbid Him to apply His mercy. He is, in fact, fully merciful and fully just.

When we take into account God's other attributes of goodness, mercy, love and grace; there are those who might make the mistake of saying that God is too kind to punish the ungodly. However, to believe this means we nullify the reality of His infinite, unchanging justice. God is the same, past present and future. He never changes. And, He cannot look upon sin. So, obviously He cannot allow sin into His Holy Kingdom. Therefore, God will have justice for sin. Either from Christ's atoning death, or, for those who will not accept that free gift of salvation, eternal wrath in hell.

R. C. Sproul once said, "Let's assume that all men are guilty of sin in the sight of God. From the mass of humanity, God sovereignly decides to give mercy to some of them. What do the rest get? They get justice. The saved get mercy and the unsaved get justice. Nobody gets injustice."

"The Rock, His work is perfect, for all His ways are justice. A God of faithfulness and without iniquity, just and upright is He." Deuteronomy 32:4

GOD IS WISE - He is Wisdom Incarnate

Let's face it. Wisdom is more than just intelligence and head knowledge. A truly wise person makes it a point to know all the facts in order to make the best decisions. Being wise means using your heart, mind and soul together with competence and the skill necessary to come up with the best solution. But, no matter what, the wisest person on earth could never come close to being as wise as God.

God is infinitely, consistently and perfectly

wise. Tozer writes, "Wisdom, among other things, is the ability to devise perfect ends and to achieve those ends by the most perfect means. It sees the end from the beginning, so there can be no need to guess or conjecture. Wisdom sees everything in focus, each in proper relation to all, and is thus able to work toward predestined goals with flawless precision."

The fact that God can never be more wise than He already is, means He is always doing what is best for our lives. When we see wisdom like this, we understand how our own limited, finite wisdom can never compare with the limitless, infinite wisdom of God. Understanding that no plans we would ever contrive, could possibly compare with the plans He has already implemented for us, is not only comforting, but immensely calming, in this crazy upside down world. We may not always understand His ways today, but we can trust Him and know that He is working all things out for our good.

"Oh, the depth of the riches and wisdom and knowledge of God! How unsearchable are His judgments and how inscrutable His ways." Romans 11:33

"And we know that for those who love God all things work together for good, for those who are called according to His purpose." Romans 8:28

GOD IS IMMUTABLE - He Does Not Ever Change

This is, and should be, a source of joy for all believers. God is dependable! We know that He will not; no, indeed cannot; change. His promises are sure, and His purposes are unfailing.

Isn't it wonderful that our trust in Him is secure? It is because the God who promised us eternal life, with Him, is immutable that we can rest assured that nothing, not trouble or hardship or persecution or famine or nakedness or danger or sword shall separate us from the love of Christ. And, it is because Jesus Christ is the same yesterday, today and forever that neither angels nor demons, neither the present nor the future, not even powers, height, depth, or anything else in all of creation, will be able to separate us from the love of God that is in Christ Jesus our Lord.

God does not change. Who He is never changes. From before the beginning of time and into eternity His character never changes. His plans do not change, and His promises never change.

"For I the Lord do not change; therefore you, O children of Jacob, are not consumed." Malachi 3:6

GOD IS FAITHFUL - He is Unflinchingly, Infinitely True

As with all of His attributes, His faithfulness is not a separate, isolated trait, but is interconnected with all parts of His perfect being. Therefore, His faithfulness cannot be understood apart from His immutability, or unchanging nature. When we say that God remains faithful, for He cannot deny Himself, we see these attributes working perfectly together. The fact that He is unchanging, means that He can never, not be faithful.

God may be safely relied upon in all things and in all areas of our lives. No one in history ever yet trusted Him in vain. God is true. His

Word of promise is sure. In His relations with His people He has always been faithful. In reading the scriptures we find over and over the precious truth that He is dependable, because His people need to know that faithfulness is an essential part of His divine nature, and that we can certainly have confidence in Him.

The fact that God is unchangeably faithful also means He never forgets anything, never changes His mind, never fails to keep a promise, or to finish anything He has set out to do. His faithfulness pours out from His unending love, so we know that we can trust Paul's word that *"in all things God works for the good of those who love Him"*.

Now, of course, in our limited understanding and finite, human minds, we don't always see 'how' His plan is faithful. Sometimes His faithfulness can even seem like abandonment, when we can't see the end from the beginning as He can. So, when it feels like you are alone, like God has left you to suffer by yourself, to hurt, or even to die? We can take comfort in knowing the true attributes of God, and that He will never leave or forsake us. Trusting faithfully in who God says He is can be a great comfort.

"Know therefore that the Lord your God is God, the faithful God who keeps covenant and steadfast love with those who love Him and keep His commandments, to a thousand generations," Deuteronomy 7:9

"The saying is trustworthy, for: If we have died with Him, we will also live with Him; if we endure, we will also reign with Him; if we deny Him, He

will also deny us; If we are faithless, He remains faithful - for He cannot deny Himself." 2 Timothy 2:11-13

GOD IS GOOD - Forever Filled With Good Will and Kindness

God's goodness, just like His other attributes, exists within His immutability. As part of His infinite and unchangeable nature, He is always good. He takes holy pleasure in seeing His people happy. His mercy flows freely from His goodness, and He is inclined to bless abundantly those He loves.

I find it somewhat amusing that, as humans, we find it much easier to agree that God is good when our lives are going well; but begin to question His goodness toward us when things take a nosedive into the difficult. We are fickle creatures.

"Oh, taste and see that the Lord is good! Blessed is the man who takes refuge in Him! Psalm 34:8

GOD IS HOLY - He is Unchangeably, Infinitely Perfect in Every Way

The definition of the word 'holy' is: sacred; consecrated; hallowed; sanctified; venerated; revered; reverenced; divine; religious; blessed; blest; dedicated. I find that no one, or even combination, of these words adequately describes the awesome holiness of our God.

Of all the characteristics of God, holiness is the one that comes closest to describing Him, and yet, in reality is a summation of all His other traits. The word holiness actually refers to His separateness, His otherness, it defines the fact that He is unlike any other being. It points to

His complete and infinite perfection. And in fact holiness binds all His other attributes together.

That God is holy means He is always perfect. And, His standard for us is perfection. *"Therefore you are to be perfect, as your Heavenly Father is perfect,"* This is exactly why we need Jesus. Without Christ having taken our place, dying for our sins and rising again, we would all fall short of God's holy standard.

God's first concern for His universe and His people is moral health, and holiness. And, let's face it, we can't get there on our own. So to preserve His creation He must destroy anything that is contrary to His plan. This is why He came, in the man Jesus, to destroy sin and death. It may seem, sometimes, as if God is angry and judgmental. But, every wrathful judgment in the history of the universe has been an act of holy preservation. God's holiness, wrath and the health of His creation are inextricably linked

Thankfully, as Christians, we will never have to experience God's holy wrath poured out. Due to Jesus' death and resurrection, the penalty for our sins has been paid and we have been credited with Christ's righteousness. Now when God looks at you, if you are born again, He sees the blood, the holiness of His one and only Son, Jesus.

"And the four living creatures, each of them with six wings, are full of eyes all around and within, and day and night they never cease to say, "Holy, holy, holy, is the Lord God Almighty, who was and is and is to come." Revelation 4:8

GOD IS SELF-SUFFICIENT - He Has No Needs

It's hard to imagine not having any need. As limited humans we have incredible needs, which if left unmet will surely result in death. God has no need. He is perfect and complete within His own being.

Because God is self-sufficient, we can go to Him with all our needs. We never have to worry about Him running out, or His abundance drying up. His never ending stores of peace, mercy, goodness and grace are available to us at all times.

"For as the Father has life in Himself, so He has granted the Son also to have life in Himself." John 5:26

But the fruit of the Spirit is love, joy, peace, patience, kindness, goodness, faithfulness, gentleness, self-control, against such things there is no law.

Galatians 5:22,23

WHO DOES THE WORLD SAY WE ARE?

As Christians, what exactly should we be striving for? Should we be striving as the world strives, trying to be popular among the masses in this decadent, deceptive culture; or working toward a life that more closely emulates that of Christ? Well, clearly, we don't have to be Rhodes Scholars to answer this one. However, even as the answer to this question is obvious, we see all around us those who profess to be Christians, but seem to care more about what the world thinks of them, than they care about what God thinks.

To be a professing Christian is one thing,

but to be a possessing Christian is quite another. Someday I will stand before the throne of God to make an account of my life here on earth. I have trusted Jesus as Savior and Lord, so I know my name is contained in 'The Lamb's Book of Life'. That, and that alone, determines my salvation and my place in heaven.

However, there were many years of my past for which I was formerly, and deeply ashamed. That is, until I trusted Jesus for salvation and His sacrifice wiped those sins away. I don't only profess to being a Christian. I own my right to claim His promises and the powers He has given me as a disciple. I am a possessing Christian, because I possess the Holy Spirit. The Spirit of the Living God lives IN ME! Wow, what a powerful and defining statement! Someday, when I do indeed stand before the throne of God, and make an accounting of what I have done since becoming a follower of Christ, I want to be able to tell my Father that I loved as He loves, and that I shared the Gospel with all those seekers He placed in my path. I long to hear those precious words, "Well done, good and faithful servant".

I truly, and sadly, spent many, many years concerned a great deal about what others thought of me. More so than I cared about what the Lord thought about me. I don't want to live with regret, and there's nothing I can do to change those years that have gone by. But, now, when God places a person in my path who does not know Him, I share the knowledge I have to the best of my ability. And, can I tell you, from personal experience, there is no better feeling in the world than to see someone's life changed by coming to know the Lord. I cry whenever a new member is added to the kingdom.

Are you a professor, or a possessor? Do you long to share the 'Good News' with everyone you meet? Do you lead by an attitude of godliness? I once heard a question posed that went something like this. "If the world was putting you on trial for being a Christian. Would they have enough proof to convict?"

How can we be more like Jesus? Embodying the fruits of the Spirit, with His help, is a good place to start. And, what are those fruits we would hope to emulate? Let us examine.

Love - *"Love is patient and kind; love does not envy or boast; it is not arrogant or rude. It does not insist on its own way; it is not irritable or resentful;*

it does not rejoice at wrongdoing, but rejoices with the truth. Love bears all things, believes all things, hopes all things, endures all things." 1 Corinthians 13:4-7

"Above all, keep loving one another earnestly, since love covers a multitude of sins." 1 Peter 4:8

I don't know how I would expound on this fruit any better than the scriptures have done for me. Except to say, there are so many people out there who just need a kind word, a hug, a word of encouragement. I want to be that person who reaches out. Remember that Jesus said they would know us by our love, and that we should love the way He has loved us. Let us all open our hearts to share the love of Christ with everyone He puts in our path.

Joy - *"Rejoice in the Lord always; and again I*

will say, Rejoice." Philippians 4:4

"Rejoice always, pray without ceasing, give thanks in all circumstances; for this is the will of God in Christ Jesus for you." 1 Thessalonians 5:16-18

"May the God of hope fill you with all joy and peace in believing, so that by the power of the Holy Spirit you may abound in hope." Romans 15:13

So many great scriptures about love and joy! I could fill pages. Notice in the second and third scriptures I've listed here that along with rejoicing Paul tells us to pray without ceasing, to give thanks in all circumstances (which is a bit different than giving thanks 'for' all circumstances) and to believe so that you may abound in hope. These are all key elements involved in the ability to rejoice.

Attitude is so important. I don't believe

we can experience true joy without regular conversations with the Father, through Jesus Christ our intercessor; without being thankful for His nearness in all situations and circumstances; or without believing in the power of Almighty God to protect and care for us. But, we are told that if we do these things we will also have hope. What better to fill our hearts with joy, than the hope that comes from the indwelling of the Holy Spirit?

Peace - *"You keep him in perfect peace whose mind is stayed on You, because he trusts in You." Isaiah 26:3*

"Do not be anxious about anything, but in everything by prayer and supplication with thanksgiving let your requests be made known to God. And the peace of God, which surpasses all

understanding, will guard your hearts and your minds in Christ Jesus." Philippians 4:6,7

"And let the peace of Christ rule in your hearts, to which indeed you were called in one body. And be thankful." Colossians 3:15

Peace can be tricky. The world around us confounds the mind and tempts the flesh at every turn. However, if our hearts are focused on the Prince of Peace and His Word, instead of the baubles and lights, He will give us the peace we so desire. As I grow older I find that the temptations of the world are no longer as tempting as they once were; and the face of Jesus comes more sharply into focus. I wish that had been the case when I was younger (again, imagine here a list of stupid things I've done). However, it remains a choice even now, and I choose peace.

I have to say that it has never been easy for any generation to grow up as a Christian on this earthly plane, but as time goes on, Satan has honed his skills to a finer, sharper, edge than ever before. We are assaulted by wickedness called inclusiveness on every side. Men who think they are women, and women who think they are men. We are assailed with evil at every turn. Rampant new abortion laws and states pushing for more euthanasia rights. Religious persecution of Christians around the world at the highest rate in history.

I urge you to reach out to young people and share the one Truth that will give them their only hope of eternity with the Father. Help them to have the peace and hope they will need in order to stand firm against our enemy, Satan.

Patience - *"Here is a call for the endurance of the saints, those who keep the commandments of God and their faith in Jesus." Revelation 14:12*

"Be still before the Lord and wait patiently for Him; fret not yourself over the one who prospers in his way, over the man who carries out evil devices." Psalm 37:7

"The Lord is not slow to fulfill His promise as some count slowness, but is patient toward you, not wishing that any should perish, but that all should reach repentance." 2 Peter 3:9

Wow. Patience. Not my strong suit. But, through the Lord, I am getting better. I guess I spent my childhood and my years as a young woman praying prayers that never seemed (in my estimation) to be answered. I got tired of waiting. I assumed God didn't care. I even blamed Him for everything wrong in my life. So much wasted time on my part.

If I had only known then. Known that it wasn't all about me. If I had only known to pray for things that would glorify God, and magnify His name. But, I was a little caught up feeling sorry for myself. You know how that goes. Or, maybe you don't. I haven't walked a mile in your shoes, so I can only assume you have gone through some things in your life that caught you off guard; some things that hurt; or even some things that broke your heart.

I have learned to trust Him. Oh, not that I never get a little impatient, but now I know that He loves me, just like He loves you, and I can depend on Him to keep His promises.

Trust Him with all your heart. He will never

let you down.

Kindness - *"Love is patient and kind;" 1 Corinthians 13:4a*

"A man who is kind benefits himself, but a cruel man hurts himself."

"Be kind to one another, tenderhearted, forgiving one another, as God in Christ forgave you." Ephesians 4:32

Kindness. Do we even remember what that is anymore? This is something the world could use a lot more of these days. I believe many suffer from the, "Well, he did it first", syndrome. I have discovered that social media is a dangerous place, especially for those of us who espouse conservative principals and views. Whatever happened to free speech? I don't have to agree with everything you believe in order to love you and be kind to you.

We are more likely to draw people to Christ with kindness, than with anger and temper tantrums. Be kind to one another for heaven's sake.

Goodness - *"Who is wise and understanding among you? By his good conduct let him show his works in the meekness of wisdom." James 3:13*

"Remember not the sins of my youth or my transgressions; according to your steadfast love remember me, for the sake of your goodness, O Lord!" Psalm 25:7

"Surely goodness and mercy shall follow me all the days of my life, and I shall dwell in the house of the Lord forever." Psalm 23:6

God is good. Me, not so much. He's helping me work on it though. Part of the problem is that I spent so much of my life thinking I could never be good enough, no matter how hard I tried, that I gave up. That was the problem all along. I was trying to do it by myself, and not including God in the process. Then, after I married Pastor Marty, I think I believed I'd achieved some kind of goodness by osmosis, and boy o boy did I spend some time acting like it. If you met me during that period of time in my life, please accept my sincerest apologies. I have since discovered that it is not possible to be good enough, except through Jesus Christ. He suffered, died and rose again to make me good enough, holy enough, and righteous enough through Him. All Him. Only Him.

Faithfulness - *"A faithful man will abound with blessings, but whoever hastens to be rich will not go unpunished." Proverbs 29:20*

"For we walk by faith, not by sight." 2 Corinthians 5:7

"Many a man proclaims his own steadfast love, but a faithful man who can find." Proverbs 20:6

What is faith? Faith is believing in something when you have no absolute proof that it even exists. Faith is scary. A faithful person knows that they know that they know that God exists, that He loves us, that He sent His Son to sacrifice Himself for our sin, that His promises are real, and that they can take Him at His Word. God and I had to spend quite some time working on this one before it grew in my heart. But, I can say with confidence that I wholly trust God now, and I have never felt as free and at peace than I do at this point in my life. God is good, and He will help you have the faith to put your trust in Him.

Gentleness - *"A soft answer turns away wrath,*

but a harsh word stirs up anger." Proverbs 15:1

"Let your reasonableness be known to everyone. The Lord is at hand." Philippians 4:5

"To speak evil of no one, to avoid quarreling, to be gentle, and to show perfect courtesy toward all people." Titus 3:2

I didn't grow up around any gentle people. The closest I ever came to gentleness as a child was my Kindergarten teacher, Miss Hoppo. I adored her. I was four years old, and small for my age. I'd begun school early, due to the fact that I was already an avid reader, and way ahead of my peers in a number of other subjects (back in those days no one took into consideration whether or not an individual was socially ready). She tended to keep me under her protective wing while I was at school. We were preparing for a

Kindergarten circus, and I was chosen to be the tight rope walker (of course the tight rope would be on the ground). I was elated.

I was to wear a one piece, wonderfully glittery, bathing suit affair, with fluff attached at the backside for added effect. But once she tried the costume on me, and saw the bruises on my back, the backs of my arms, and the backs of my thighs, she decided she couldn't let me wear that costume where others might see evidence of the abuse I'd suffered. I did not know this. She told me someone else had been chosen for my role, and my heart was broken. However I contracted measles before the circus, and missed the whole thing anyway, so she might as well have held off. I never would have known.

She went to my mother to try and get

some answers. The answers she got were not satisfactory, and she attempted to intervene with help from the authorities. The problem with that solution was that back in the dark ages, when I was a child, there was no organization called child protective services. A man's wife and children were essentially his property and authorities hesitated to get involved in cases like mine. When I came back to school after my absence, Miss Hoppo was no longer my teacher. I spent several years thinking she just didn't like me anymore and I was crushed. But I was used to this kind of reaction, so I simply stored it away in my mind, in the 'reasons for lack of self confidence' file. When I grew older, my curiosity got the better of me and I looked her up. She was able to tell me everything about what had happened during that time, and we cried together over the phone.

Since my biological father's family was very prominent in the town where I grew up, even though we didn't personally benefit from that family prominence, they got what they wanted. She had been removed to another Kindergarten class where I couldn't have contact with her. When she tried to report my father, she was warned that she would lose her job if she tried to speak to me again. Evil is ugly, so it hides. And when the eyes of the world are closed and heads are turned away it is usually the weakest among us who struggle and lose.

I try very hard, with the help of the Lord, to be that soft place to fall for my husband, kids and grandkids. There is so much that is not gentle in this world in which we live. This past Mother's

Day, my young grandson wrote me a note. It made me cry. He thanked me for loving them unconditionally and for always being so gentle with them no matter what. That would certainly be a God thing. And I am thankful that He is so very good to us.

Self-Control - *"The end of all things is at hand; therefore be self-controlled and sober-minded for the sake of your prayers." 1 Peter 4:7*

"Whoever is slow to anger is better than the mighty, and he who rules his spirit than he who takes a city." Proverbs 16:32

"A man without self-control is like a city broken into and left without walls." Proverbs 25:28

Self-Control is a hard one for some. When people come to me and tell me they can't control themselves, that anger runs in their family, and that once they get going they can't stop. Or when they espouse that this is just who they are, it breaks my heart. We all have the ability to control ourselves, with God's help. The problem is that many try to do it on their own. And just like any of the fruits of the Spirit, these traits depend on the Spirit to bring results. You are right if you declare that YOU can't do it. Because you were never meant to do it on your own. Pray for God to walk with you in this. Begin each day in some time alone with the Lord. Start your day off with prayer.

I am told quite frequently, by those very same folks wanting to know how to live their lives in peace, that they don't have time to pray in the morning. Too much to do. Too busy and rushed. I used to think that as well. That is, until

I began to spend time with God first thing in the mornings. A little at first. Maybe only a scripture or two and a page of devotion. That grew into more scriptures and study, more devotionals and more meditation. Now, when I pray in the mornings, I am loath to quit. I would rather be in communion with the Lord, than any other place in the universe. And, do you want to know the thing I have discovered about spending the first part of your day with Him? I have discovered that if you start the day with Jesus, He will make sure you have time for everything else you need to do.

Self-Control isn't just that thing which helps you keep your mouth shut when you're feeling angry. It is also the trait that will help you organize your day, finish tasks you've put off for too long, learn how to get along better with others, and create time to study the Word.

And we know that for those who love God all things work together for good, for those who are called according to His purpose. For those whom He foreknew He also predestined to be conformed to the image of His Son, in order that He might be the first born among many brothers. And those whom He predestined He also called, and whom He called He also justified, and those whom He justified He also glorified.

Romans 8:28-30

CONFORMED TO THE IMAGE OF HIS SON

"So whether you eat or drink, or whatever you do, do all to the glory of God. Give no offence to Jews or to Greeks or to the church of God just as I try to please everyone in everything I do, not seeking my own advantage, but that of many, that they may be saved. Be imitators of me, as I am of Christ." 1 Corinthians 10:31-33

You might wonder how we are supposed to get to a place where we can make a statement like the one Paul made. Well, I'm here to tell you that if you are an imperfect, sinful person, relying on the perfect Grace of God, the redeeming power of the sacrifice of Jesus, and the power of the Holy Spirit to guide you, you are moving in the right direction.

For me, it feels a bit pretentious to make that statement. Due to the fact that I seem to continue messing up on a daily basis. But, I've grown by leaps and bounds compared to where I was at the time I was diagnosed with stage 4 cancer and given a three to six month life expectancy in October of 2010. Back then I thought my sanctity had something to do with how worthy I was on my own, and I was abundantly aware that if I died I would be in hell for eternity. But, what to do? Through a series of events that I laid out in my first book, "When All Else Fails, God's Grace and the Power of Prayer", I came to know that God's Grace didn't have anything at all to do with how good I was on my own.

I discovered that Jesus' sacrifice on the cross paid it all. When He cried out, "It is Finished", He meant He'd paid it all; our debt for sin, for sickness and disease, for emotional pain, and for every other human condition known to mankind.

Through reading and studying scripture I came to know that I can never be righteous on my own; which was a huge relief to me since I didn't seem to be making any headway in that direction (whew!); and that in Christ I am covered by His righteousness. I am under His blood, justified by His redeeming actions. Praise God that He makes a way, through faith, to reward those who seek Him.

"And without faith it is impossible to please Him, for whoever would draw near to God must

believe that He exists and that He rewards those who seek Him." Hebrews 11:6

So, how do I conform to the image of His Son? I can't be perfect, no matter how hard I try or how much I work at it, and Jesus is perfect.

Dear one, the moment you put on Christ you are covered in such a way that when the Father sees you, all He sees is His beautiful Son.

So then, if I am covered, and the Father sees only the Son, and I'm going to heaven anyway, then why do I care about conforming? I mean, really, in the sixties and seventies when we used to march around protesting, everything, that word, 'conforming' was the enemy. Why would I want to conform now? And, how does it help anyone if I do?

Now that we have trusted Jesus for Salvation,

it means very little if we are refusing to make Him the Lord of our life. And here is the reason for that. Yes, if you were serious in your crying out to Him and you really meant that you wanted Him to save you and live in you, you are assured a place in heaven when you die.

However, if you refuse to make Him Lord of your life, choosing to do your own selfish thing throughout your earthly life, instead of His gracious thing, you will spend many fruitless, unproductive and horrid worldly days until the appointed time for you to leave this earth and be with Him. I am always a bit suspect of someone who declares that they want Jesus as their Savior, but fights Him tooth and nail. Did that individual really want a Savior, or did they just want fire insurance?

You see, our eternity actually begins the moment we are joined spiritually with Him. And, yes, you have the opportunity to fill that time with peace and infinite joy, right here on earth by following Him during the time you have left. Now, that doesn't mean you won't still have troubles, no one is guaranteed that. Even Jesus had troubles on earth. But, it does mean you will be better able to face those troubles knowing you have a God who cares and all His armies of Heavenly Host backing you up! If we are not interested in making Jesus Christ the Lord of our lives, we might ask ourselves, was I serious about wanting to follow Him, or was this merely a fleeting fad?

If we are serious about our commitment to follow Christ, then we will necessarily want to present an example to others that draws them to the Father. For if that is not our goal, perhaps we should examine our motives in asking Him into our lives in the first place. Considering that going into all the world and sharing the Gospel, to make disciples, is one of the two commands that He left for us; I would say that should be a priority going forward, wouldn't you?

So, since I'm not Jesus, but merely a disciple, how am I qualified for such a daunting task? Yes I know I'm covered by the blood. Yes, I'm righteous in Him. Yes, we are to love one another as He has loved us. But, what about the rest of it? How do I conform in order to be any earthly, or heavenly, good to those He sets before me?

That my friends is where learning the characteristics of a godly life will come in handy.

Along with the merits of the fruits of the Spirit, these godly characteristics will help you achieve a nature (with God's help and timing) that will work toward bringing others to saving Grace in Christ Jesus. Since what we do is a direct result of who we believe we are, and what we are is determined by our values. Then our values determine our character, and our character determines our behavior.

As a follower of Christ we want to be an example for others to follow. So, we should ask ourselves a few questions:

When people spend time with me, do they go away desiring the things of the world: wealth, material possessions, fame, sexual pleasure or popularity, just to mention a few; or do they desire to be more like Christ?

Do the characteristics reflected by my life demonstrate the world's values; or do they reflect the values of Christ?

What values and characteristics do people want to learn and emulate by observing my character?

"I appeal to you therefore, brothers, by the mercies of God, to present your bodies as a living sacrifice, holy and acceptable to God, which is your spiritual worship. Do not be conformed to this world, but be transformed by the renewal of your mind, that by testing you may discern what is the will of God, what is good and acceptable and perfect." Romans 12:1,2

What follows is a list of characteristics, which are based on the principle that God has a purpose for each and every believer once they become a disciple of Jesus Christ. Are we exemplifying these traits in our everyday life?

*As a believer in Jesus Christ; someone who knows Jesus as my personal Lord and savior; am I sharing His Love, His Grace and the message of His Gospel at every opportunity?

*Do I demonstrate to the world, since I believe that I am controlled and sanctioned by the Holy Spirit, what it is to be an empowered emissary of the Lord?

*Am I exhibiting a victorious life, as one who has Christ's authority over all the enemy's power?

*Do I leave my house each day wearing God's armor, clothed in all I need to defeat Satan?

*Do I do my best to keep myself physically pure, as a way to honor God with every part of my body?

*Am I love motivated? Do I love my family

and others more than I love myself?

*Am I secure in the love of God, knowing that in Christ I am extremely valued?

*Am I living as a self-confident person, or a God-confident person, knowing from where my help comes?

*Do I have a servant heart? Or, do I expect others to continually serve me? Remember Jesus washing the feet of His disciples.

*Do I do my best each day for the glory of God, in the workplace, at home, in my community?

*Do I trust in God's provision? Am I secure in the knowledge that He supplies all my needs according to His riches and not mine?

*Do I live a purposeful life? Do I live my life in accordance with God's plans for me, and not by one accident after another?

Now, having said all that. Are you going to be welcomed with open arms in every venue where you want to speak of Christ? No. Is it possible that you will be persecuted, ridiculed, harassed, excluded, or even slain for your belief in Christ and for trying to share the Gospel with others? That, especially in the times we live, is a distinct possibility. But, is it worth it to share the love of Jesus? Oh yes my friend. Yes, yes, yes a million times yes. And though you may even be persecuted in arenas, which you supposed to be Christian, for simply speaking the truth. You will have rewards in heaven. Don't be surprised when these things happen, because I am warning you now. Continue to do good, though the world persecute you.

"Beloved, do not be surprised at the fiery trial

when it comes upon you to test you, as though something strange were happening to you. But rejoice insofar as you share Christ's sufferings, that you may also rejoice and be glad when His glory is revealed. If you are insulted for the name of Christ, you are blessed, because the Spirit of glory and of God rests upon you. But let none of you suffer as a murderer or a thief or an evildoer or as a meddler. Yet if anyone suffers as a Christian, let him not be ashamed, but let him glorify God in that name. For it is time for judgment to begin at the household of God; and if it begins with us, what will be the outcome for those who do not obey the Gospel of God? And if the righteous is scarcely saved, what will become of the ungodly and the sinner? Therefore let those who suffer according to God's will entrust their souls to a faithful Creator while doing good."

1Peter 4:12-19

Humble yourselves, therefore, under the mighty hand of God so that at the proper time He may exalt you, casting all your anxieties on Him, because He cares for you. Be sober-minded; be watchful. Your adversary the devil prowls around like a roaring lion, seeking someone to devour. Resist him, firm in your faith, knowing that the same kinds of suffering are being experienced by your brotherhood throughout the world. And after you have suffered a little while, the God of all Grace, who has called you to His eternal glory in Christ, will Himself restore, confirm, strengthen, and establish you"
1Peter 5:6-10

How then will they call on Him in whom they have not believed? And how are they to believe in Him of whom they have never heard? And how are they to hear without someone preaching? And how are they to preach unless they are sent? As it is written, "How beautiful are the feet of those who preach the good news!" But they have not all obeyed the Gospel. For Isaiah says, "Lord, who has believed what he has heard from us?" So, faith comes by hearing, and hearing through the Word of Christ.

Romans 10:14-17

HOW SHALL THEY HEAR?

I want to reach the world with the Gospel, don't you? I want everyone to know Jesus, don't you? Excited about a new book being released, I asked these questions of an acquaintance recently. I was surprised at the reply. And, I must say, very saddened. This individual, who'd always referred to herself as a Christian said, "What difference does it make? I can't be the world's religious conscience, and it's not like they listen anyway. Besides, there are people who will kill you if you say your religion is better than theirs."

Okay, the getting killed part is pretty scary.

And, there are actually many countries where the laws are so strict (most Muslim nations for instance) that you can be imprisoned, or even killed, for proselytizing. But, we're still supposed to share The Savior, aren't we?

Jesus never said it would be easy to share the Gospel. Satan is in it to win it after all. Now, we do know how the story ends, and we win, but that doesn't mean the devil is going down without a fight, so we have to be willing to stand firm against him.

I was serious when I said I want everyone to know Jesus. I know that's what God wants too. I know because I saw it in 2 Peter 3:9, which reads: "*The Lord is not slow to fulfill His promise as some count slowness, but is patient toward you, not wishing that any should perish, but that all should reach repentance."* The Word of God is replete with scripture telling us that God wants us to reach everyone with the message of saving grace.

If you are a Christian, you should want everyone to know Him too. But, how do we do that? I'm getting old. Due to a number of surgeries, and some current medications with particular side effects, I don't get around as well as I used to. So, how do I take the Gospel to the nations? Well, there are lots of ways we can make that happen. I write, in hopes that my books will deliver the message of God's grace. I've even had a few international sales!

Praise God for missionaries! They are on the front lines of worldwide evangelism, and we couldn't do it without them, so my husband and I give to missionaries through our church, and also to several organizations outside of our church, that support worldwide missions.

But, there are many right here in our country, as strange as that may sound to believers, who don't know Jesus. How, you might ask, can anyone who lives in the USA, with Bibles available everywhere, including on line, and even apps for your phone, not know Jesus? Again, I will say, Satan.

A Barna Research study conducted by two consecutive surveys, one in 2014, and one in 2015, had some interesting results.

Though Jesus Christ has appeared in hundreds of pop culture places, from Da Vinci Code to South Park; and has been fictionalized, satirized, and mythologized over the centuries, the majority of Americans still believe Him to be a historical figure. That is good news. However, the numbers decline with each new generation. When we read that 96% of Elders, 95% of Boomers, 91% of Gen-Xers, and then only 87% of Millennials believe that Jesus was a real person who actually lived and walked on the earth, we are starting to see a downward spiral that is frightening. And, many of those think He was merely a prophet, a missionary of sorts, or even just a really nice guy with some good ideas.

Some of the additional results are even more disturbing. Only 48% of Millennials believe that Jesus is God. When those who believed He was a real person were asked if Jesus was sinless? Only 52% believed He is without sin. There is also a significant difference in what makes up the bulk of believers. Of women, 68% claim to be Christ followers; but for men the numbers were only 56%. For Black Americans, 80% declare Christ as Lord, for Hispanics the number dropped to 65% and then a paltry 60% of White Americans, (which to me was a sad showing), claimed to follow Jesus.

Income appears to be a significant factor as well. More than 65% of those making less than $50,000 a year answered yes to the question, when asked if they were Christian believers. The number dropped to 63% for those in the $50,000 - $100,000 range, and only 53% of those making over $100,000 claimed to follow Christ. So, I guess many who have money don't think they need Jesus too.

When asked if they had made a personal commitment to follow Christ; Elders had done so by 71%, Boomers were at 65%, Gen-Xers at 59%, and Sadly, Millennials at a pathetic 46%.

Astonishingly, when queried on how we get to heaven? There appeared to be a huge misperception. Many, even some of those who claimed to be followers of Jesus, believed they would get to heaven by the number of good deeds they performed. And worse, some of those who said they had trusted in Jesus as Savior, still didn't believe they would end up in heaven when they died. Wow!

I guess that means we aren't making a very big impact in America, huh? You know, when Marty and I were ministering at a large church in Sioux City, Iowa, some years ago; we had an experience that might highlight this trend. A missionary couple, from Guatemala, came to our church and wanted help with a missions project they were involved in around the area. It seemed they'd been sent here, to the United States of America, to bring the message of the Gospel to the lost. I was thrown for a loop that, at least in their country, 'everyone' knew America was becoming a more godless nation year by year. I find that sad, don't you? America used to be a country that sent missionaries all around the globe in order to share Jesus. And now those countries feel the need to share Jesus with us.

Pretty simply, we as the church have not been doing enough to bring others to the knowledge of Christ Jesus and His saving Grace. How have we come to this? Through decades of pressure to take God out of every aspect of our lives; and deciding that we didn't want to 'push our religion on everyone else'. That's how. Who came up with that anyway? Well, the answer again is, Satan. Do you remember during the sixties and seventies; 'free love', peace symbols, long hair and bell-bottomed pants? When so many young people decided if they ever had kids they weren't going to make them follow their parent's religion, but would allow them to make up their own minds once they reached adulthood? Whose idea do you think that was?

So, those young people grew up; got married, or didn't; had children; and proceeded to raise them without Jesus. Many of those children, and their 'religion' contrary parents, are the ones who march around, hollering and shouting that God doesn't belong in our schools, our government, or our town square.

Now many of those young people who were born in the eighties and nineties and beyond are having kids, married or not. And, when asked their opinions about Jesus, they don't seem to know much of anything about who He is, or what He's done for us. In many cases it isn't that they hate God. They just don't know who He is. No one ever introduced them. I've actually heard tell about some exciting revivals starting up among teens. We will have to keep an eye on that and see what God is doing.

Those 'Freedom from Religion' people who were spawned from a desperation to be free from responsibility to a higher power (you know, the whole "if it feels good do it" era); have no idea that Jesus isn't about religion, He is about relationships with His children, even those of us who are not perfect.

We must step up and begin boldly sharing the Gospel. We can no longer assume that everyone around us knows the Lord. Just because we live in a country where we are free (at least for now) to worship as we please, does not mean that everyone is following the Lord. And, I might also note that many who are worshipping, are venerating a false God.

In ideologies such as Islam, or religions like Buddhism, Daoism, Hinduism, etc., adherents are not reaching out to Jehovah God, but a false God. We have become so 'politically correct' that we are afraid to step on anyone's toes by introducing Jesus into the mix. Well, folks, those people who do not profess Christ as Savior will not go to heaven. The Bible is very clear that Jesus is the 'Only Way' to the Father. I for one can't just sit by. I will share my Lord with EVERYONE that He places in my path, politically correct or not.

I spoke with a woman at a vendor's market where I had a booth set up for my books. She was walking by, doing her best to ignore me for the most part. I stepped forward with one of my book marks. She pulled back as if I was trying to hand her a viper. I told her it was only a free book mark, so she took it and looked as if she might just move on. Then she turned and asked me what kind of books I write.

I told her I'm a stage 4 cancer survivor, and that my journey had led me to a wonderful relationship with the Lord, so now I write novels about the redemptive, and healing power of God. She chuckled and asked me if I really believed all that stuff, and I assured her I did. She didn't buy a book that day, but at a later speaking engagement for a women's group she approached me and told me she had ordered one of my books online after visiting my website, and was coming to get another. She told me I had made her question her non-belief, and that she was currently 'thinking' about a few things. I hope God uses this opportunity to touch her heart.

We are living in very dark times. I have heard it said that the end is near, and Jesus will be coming back soon. As humans, we don't know when that time might be, but we are supposed to be prepared for it at all times.

With many advocating for the elimination of all mention of God, everywhere we go, we must be a light in these darkened times. We must be strong and brave, not letting Satan have his evil way any longer. Take up your standard and march for what is right. March for Jesus.

"You are the light of the world. A city set on a hill cannot be hidden. Nor do people light a lamp and put it under a basket, but on a stand, and it gives light to all in the house. In the same way, let your light shine before others, so that they may see your good works and give glory to your Father who is in heaven." Matthew 5:15,16

Go and make disciples of everyone you meet. Don't be embarrassed to ask someone you come across if they know Jesus. Trust the Lord to give you the right words to say, and be bold. Phillip Yancey wrote, "I have learned that faith means trusting in advance what will only make sense in reverse."

"Have I not commanded you? Be strong and courageous. Do not be frightened, and do not be dismayed, for the Lord your God is with you wherever you go." Joshua 1:9

The soul of the wicked desires evil; his neighbor finds no mercy in his eyes.

Proverbs 21:10

GOOD IS EVIL AND EVIL IS GOOD-LOSING SIGHT OF THE HOLY TRUTH

Hey, we were warned. I look around me today and see a world that astounds me in its corruption and wickedness. Satan has done a pretty good job after all. Though he certainly had lots of help. It used to be that the church was a central part of every community. That was where we went (Not me personally, but you get my meaning). Not just for Sunday services and Bible study, but for community get-togethers, dances, and just about everything else.

Another place you could expect to see

wholesome, Christ centered teaching, was our schools and colleges. These institutions were designed not only as places of higher education, but were also organizations built upon the foundation of biblical Christianity. American colleges emphasized scriptural literacy, Christian moral principles, a biblical world view and salvation through Jesus Christ.

Puritans established Harvard College in 1636. Harvard's mission statement, given in 1642 read: "Everyone shall consider as the main end of his life and studies, to know God and Jesus Christ, which is eternal life. John 17:3" Harvard's motto, written in 1650 was, "In Christi Gloriam" ("For the Glory of Christ"). For many decades Puritan ministers served as her presidents.

Most Ivy League institutions were also

founded by Christian organizations. Connecticut Congregationalists, Yale; Presbyterians, Princeton; Baptists, Brown; and Evangelicals, Dartmouth. The founders of these schools recognized the need for a Christian influence in society and for our youth. They trained clergy, but also prepared students for careers in education, medicine, business and law.

American colleges expected independence and patriotism from their students. But, they also encouraged salvation through Christ, and the use of scripture before weighing any political considerations. Meaning, each person was to vote their Christian conscience when choosing leaders for our country.

Perhaps that is one of the ways this country has gotten so wildly off track. We have removed

God from our schools, but we have also removed common sense from our voting process. For heaven's sake. If you are pro-life, why would you vote for a candidate who is pro-abortion? If you are an advocate of marriage between a man and a woman, wouldn't you lean toward a candidate who thinks the same way? You get my meaning.

Christian educators always had a very big impact on our culture, they still do. The Rev. William McGuffey served as professor of moral philosophy at the University of Virginia. He was best known for his "McGuffey's Readers," used by millions of American school children. These readers taught more than just reading skills to children. They also taught essential elements of Christian morality and doctrine to students at the college which was founded by Thomas Jefferson.

As recently as 1924, Duke University's mission statement read, "The aims of Duke University are to assert a faith in the eternal union of knowledge and religion set forth in the teachings and character of Jesus Christ, the Son of God"

Then everything changed. Where prior to the 20th century Christian values had a necessary and expected place in our colleges and universities; over the next century these institutions abandoned or silenced the spiritual messages of their founders. Rapidly, those committed to secularism, humanism, and liberalism took over. Those who considered themselves cultural elites grew hostile to biblical Christianity. Some modernists even argue today that faith based learning institutions are antithetical to the spirit of American education.

Throughout this process, these institutions churned out graduates with a liberal world view that would become more observable as the decades marched on.

Those of us old enough saw it coming, didn't we? Where once we, who didn't know to bow our heads when the school morning began with prayer, were the ones spurned; now, most schools have a strict 'no prayer' policy.

I've never quite been able to figure out how liberals managed to get prayer out of school; or where they get the idea that our Constitution is against religion anywhere. The first amendment of the Constitution of America reads exactly this way: "Congress shall make no law respecting an establishment of religion, or prohibiting the free exercise thereof; or abridging the freedom of speech, or of the press; or the right of the people peaceably to assemble, and to petition the Government for a redress of grievances." Any sane person can see that a people who fled a land where they were forced, under penalty of law, to practice the religion of the land. Simply migrated to a place where they could practice whatever religion they wanted, or no religion at all. A place where the government couldn't tell them which religion they must adhere to, or which they must avoid.

Nowhere in that hallowed document does it say, 'separation of church and state'. But this issue is pushed relentlessly, in schools and government buildings. I have a question then, for all those who would shout "separation of church and state", from the house tops. Why is it that in recent years it has become acceptable, no, not just acceptable, but seemingly absolutely necessary, to teach Islam in more and more schools in our country? We can't mention Jesus, but liberal groups come into the schools and teach students the five pillars of Islam, pass out hijabs to the girls, and make each child choose a Muslim name. Yes, this is happening all around the country!

Good has become evil and evil good in the eyes of so many. How did we get here? Again, yep you got it, Satan. This is his job after all. We know what he's up to, and it is our job to see that he doesn't get away with it!

I believe that Satan used human nature against us, don't you? We don't want anyone to be 'the boss of us'. The Left tends to think that big government, or socialism, is the answer, that it will give them more freedoms, when in fact the opposite is true. It would actually mean more rules and less freedoms for everyone, except those in charge.

Interesting that the definition of the word Laodicea is, 'the people's rule', or what we might dub humanism. The people of this wealthy biblical city, in the book of Revelation 3:17-20, thought they had everything, when in fact they lacked the one thing which was most important; the only thing that really mattered; the Lord. God said they were neither hot, nor cold, but lukewarm. Therefore He spewed them out of His mouth.

Humanism, or the Left's desire to strip the

world of any responsibility to, or honor for a Holy God, is simply an attempt to relieve themselves of any guilt stemming from their godless actions and decisions. During these last days some want the government to give them whatever they need and absolve them of any liability for their actions. But it isn't the government's job to take care of us. It never was. The government doesn't have what we need. We need Jesus. Many on the left believe that socialism is the answer for every ill. It is not.

I talked to a person, who will remain unnamed, who is a proponent of abortion. I am vehemently against abortion, among other things, which the Lord abhors. We were having a lively conversation about some of the new laws that have passed, allowing abortion clear up until the birth of the baby. Barbaric! This person said they didn't have a problem with that, saying it should be the woman's choice of what to do with her own body. Boy that gets old.

I explained to this individual that unless she was from another planet with occupants who sport two heads, four arms and four legs, it is pretty clear that this child is not part of a woman's body. We talked more. She said that this wasn't an actual live baby. I told her that the baby's heart begins to beat at three weeks and one day, and the baby begins to suck his or her thumb at nine weeks. She said it was more like an organ than a being. I told her that she can't live without her organs, but she can live without this baby in her womb. And that this child has her own unique DNA, her own 23 pairs of chromosomes, and her very own blood type.

She said to me that there were already so many unwanted babies out there, that she wouldn't feel right bringing another one into the world. I explained that there are an average of 650,000 abortions performed in America each year, and that each year there are approximately 1,200,000 couples longing to adopt a child. That currently there are over 2,000,000 couples waiting, who would be thrilled to take that baby. Then she said that many women can't handle the financial weight of such a decision. The cost of bringing a baby into the world and all. I explained to her that there are many agencies out there waiting to help new moms with everything they need to take care of a baby, if they should only choose to keep the baby.

Then, of course, came the famous, "What if the baby is a result of rape or incest. Or what if it will pose a danger to the mother's health to have the child." I explained to her that a number of years ago abortion clinics were mandated to report to the CDC, the number of abortions they perform, and the reason given by the mother for wanting the abortion. In the most recent year of reporting, the CDC said that less than 1% of all abortions came under the heading of rape or incest, and only a portion of 1% came under the reasoning that the pregnancy would cause harm to the mother's health, or that the baby was diagnosed with genetic problems. What does that tell us? It tells us that 99% of all abortions performed fell under the heading of 'inconvenient for me to have a baby at this time'.

I told her that inconvenience hardly seemed a valid reason to murder a baby.

Her next comment made me a bit angry. "Well, no woman should be forced to carry a baby for nine months and give birth. There are lots of things that can go wrong during a pregnancy." After I calmed down a bit, I agreed with her. "You are absolutely correct. There are lots of things that can go wrong during a pregnancy and birth, and not everyone is cut out to be a mother. However, that might be something to consider before having sex. I believe that sex education is taught in all schools now, at about fifth grade level, so there is no reason for any woman not to know what causes pregnancy. Considering the fact that sex was created by a Holy God, as an act of love between a married man and woman, and not something to be perverted. Perhaps it would be a good thing if, as a society, we quit condoning it's misuse, and we might stop having so many reasons to think we need abortions.

Her last comment was a grievous indictment on our nation's rampant move away from Christianity. And a statement on how the non-believing population in this country thinks, at least in general. She said, "I don't know why this upsets you. It's not like it's against the law or anything. If a woman wants to have an abortion, she doesn't need your permission." And, sadly, she is right. So, that just about said it all. No matter how many good reasons I can come up with to explain that abortion is wrong and unnecessary, She could always come back with, It's not against the law, so it must be okay.

Now, I will admit, I probably got way to upset with this woman. And I usually try very hard to be more patient with those who clearly don't have a good understanding of the Grace of God, because it wasn't so terribly long ago that I was in that number.

She did, after all, grow up in a world that thinks it should be able to kill it's babies, and it's elderly people. A country where men are women and women are men; where public restrooms are interchangeable; and you can decide not to assign a gender to your new baby, you know, so they can choose for themselves what they are going to be later on. A country that throws away Jesus, in favor of a god that wants his followers to kill everyone that won't convert to his murderous ideology. A country that seems to think the government should support them, when in fact the government has no money except that which it takes from its people.

Yes, we are living in some pretty scary times. The urging of God's people, much like the minor prophets of old, go mostly ignored. Greed and avarice rule the day. The powerful oppress the weak. Corruption and wickedness are commonplace. People have become dissatisfied and bored with God and religion. We prioritize our own laws and morality over God's. Preaching centers only on the preferable parts of the Bible – and it has become the norm to put the words of authors and motivational speakers over God's Word. We're ignoring perils of sin. Love is reframed as "tolerance" and "political correctness." Fear of offending people keeps us from sharing God's word with others. We are molding God in our own image instead of worshipping Him as the one true God of the universe.

This might be a good time to examine ourselves. Are we hot, cold, or merely lukewarm? It will be up to us, those who love the Lord, to make sure the next generation knows of the Grace of God in the midst of all this evil. We cannot be afraid, or shy. We must be bold.

"What then? Only that in every way, whether in pretense or in truth, Christ is proclaimed, and in that I rejoice. Yes, and I will rejoice, for I know that through your prayers and the help of the Spirit of Jesus Christ this will turn out for my deliverance, as it is my eager expectation and hope that I will not be at all ashamed, but that with full courage now as always Christ will be honored in my body,

whether by life or by death. For to me, to live is Christ, and to die is gain." Philippians 1:18-21

Finally, brothers, whatever is true, whatever is honorable, whatever is just, whatever is pure, whatever is lovely, whatever is commendable, if there is any excellence, if there is anything worthy of praise, think about these things.

Philippians 4:8

THE TRUTH ABOUT YOUR ENEMY

Do you remember Paul Harvey? Absolutely one of my favorites. I loved his radio program. Many years ago he wrote a piece entitled, "If I Were the Devil" as a form of social criticism. It was an essay that postulates what steps the devil might take in order to corrupt human civilization, and the U.S. in particular, to lead it down the path of darkness — before delivering the catch that all the steps listed were phenomena already taking place. From the mid-1960s onwards he featured it on the radio, and in his newspaper column many times over the course of his long career, periodically updating it to incorporate current trends. Here is the first version I could find, written in 1964:

If I were the prince of darkness, I would want to engulf the whole world in darkness. I'd have a third of its real estate and four-fifths of its population, but I would not be happy until I had seized the ripest apple on the tree — thee.

So, I would set about however necessary to take over the United States.

I'd subvert the churches first, and I would begin with a campaign of whispers.

With the wisdom of a serpent, I would whisper to you as I whispered to Eve: "Do as you please."

To the young, I would whisper that the Bible is a myth. I would convince the children that man created God instead of the other way around. I'd confide that what's bad is good and what's good is square.

And the old, I would teach to pray after me, "Our Father, which are in Washington …"

Then, I'd get organized, I'd educate authors in how to make lurid literature exciting so that anything else would appear dull and uninteresting.

I'd peddle narcotics to whom I could. I'd sell alcohol to ladies and gentlemen of distinction. I'd tranquilize the rest with pills.

If I were the devil, I'd soon have families at war with themselves, churches at war with themselves and nations at war with themselves until each, in its turn, was consumed.

And with promises of higher ratings, I'd have mesmerizing media fanning the flames.

If I were the devil, I would encourage schools

to refine young intellect but neglect to discipline emotions. I'd tell teachers to let those students run wild. And before you knew it, you'd have drug-sniffing dogs and metal detectors at every schoolhouse door.

Within a decade, I'd have prisons overflowing and judges promoting pornography. Soon, I would evict God from the courthouse and the schoolhouse and then from the houses of Congress.

In his own churches, I would substitute psychology for religion and deify science. I'd lure priests and pastors into misusing boys and girls and church money.

If I were the devil, I'd take from those who have and give to those who wanted until I had killed the incentive of the ambitious.

What'll you bet I couldn't get whole states to promote gambling as the way to get rich?

I'd convince the young that marriage is old-fashioned, that swinging is more fun and that what you see on television is the way to be.

And thus, I could undress you in public and lure you into bed with diseases for which there are no cures.

In other words, if I were the devil, I'd just keep right on doing what he's doing.

WOW! It's hard to believe that was written in 1964, and that all those things were currently happening. But I found a later version. Some say Paul Harvey updated his essay, and others say it was an anonymous author. Either way, I thought the updates were interesting.

1999

If I were the devil . . . I would gain control of the most powerful nation in the world;

I would delude their minds into thinking that they had come from man's effort, instead of God's blessings;

I would promote an attitude of loving things and using people, instead of the other way around;

I would dupe entire states into relying on gambling for their state revenue;

I would convince people that character is not an issue when it comes to leadership;

I would make it legal to take the life of unborn babies;

I would make it socially acceptable to take one's own life, and invent machines to make it convenient;

I would cheapen human life as much as possible so that the life of animals are valued more than human beings;

I would take God out of the schools, where even the mention of His name was grounds for a lawsuit;

I would come up with drugs that sedate the mind and target the young, and I would get sports heroes to advertise them;

I would get control of the media, so that every night I could pollute the mind of every family member for my agenda;

I would attack the family, the backbone of any nation.

I would make divorce acceptable and easy, even fashionable. If the family crumbles, so does the nation;

I would compel people to express their most depraved fantasies on canvas and movie screens, and I would call it art;

I would convince the world that people are born homosexuals, and that their lifestyles should be accepted and marveled;

I would convince the people that right and wrong are determined by a few who call themselves authorities and refer to their agenda as politically correct;

I would persuade people that the church is irrelevant and out of date, and the Bible is for the naive;

I would dull the minds of Christians, and make them believe that prayer is not important, and that faithfulness and obedience are optional;

I guess I would leave things pretty much the

way they are.

Again, Wow! Quite a commentary. But that was 1999. It has been another twenty plus years, and things have only continued to roll downhill. Too bad Paul Harvey is no longer with us. We could use an update.

The thief comes only to steal and kill and destroy. I came that they may have life and have it abundantly.

> John 10:10

THE GOOD NEWS

And here it is. God sent His Son to die on a cross as a propitiation (atonement) for my sin. He suffered and died, overcame death and hell to rise again on the third day, and sits on the right hand of God the Father. If I confess that I am a sinner, and further confess that Jesus is the Son of God, that He died for me and then overcame death; then I am saved. But, I am not just saved for heaven when I die. I am saved for good works while I am here, in order to grow the Kingdom of God, and to give God the Father glory and honor. I am free. I am a child of the most High God. and I am a joint heir with Christ Jesus. Glory to God!

"The Spirit Himself bears witness with our spirit that we are children of God, and if children, then heirs - heirs of God and fellow heirs with Christ, provided we suffer with Him in order that we may also be glorified with Him." Romans 8:16,17

What a legacy, what an inheritance!

You know, I went many, many years of my life not knowing about the Love and Grace of God for me. But, I also went many, many years of my life not understanding Satan. I feared him in all the wrong ways. I didn't know, that as a follower of Christ, he didn't have any power over me except what I gave him.

Because of that my life was not full, and I was unhappy and depressed.

As I said in the beginning of this book, I don't want us to put too much focus on the enemy.

But, it is good to know what we are up against. Now, as a born again follower of Jesus, I need to equip myself.

Satan hates anyone who is trying to do good in the world, in the Name of Jesus. So, I will equip myself with the Word. I will hide it in my heart to strengthen me when the enemy attacks.

With God's help I will try not to be selfish, or complain.

With God's help I will withstand the devil; I will be firm in faith, strong, immovable and determined, so that I can be prepared when temptation comes.

Remember, dear ones, that the Word of God has the power to renew our minds, heal our sickness and brokenness, and change our very lives.

The Word of God gives us the power and the authority to conquer the devil. He hates it and he hates you, but that's okay, we don't like him anyway.

Make it a priority to spend time in the Word every day. You won't ever be sorry you did. The Bible is God's love letter to us, as His beloved children. Meditate on it, get it deep into your heart, and with His help begin to live it with conviction.

Pray, and never stop praying. Prayer works. I am a living, breathing, example of the power of prayer. Make it a part of your day, all day.

Remember beloved. You have everything you need, as a follower of Christ, to defeat Satan.

You have everything you need to live an abundant life.

You have everything you need to be full of peace and joy.

You have everything you need to remain stable.

And by the Grace of God, you have all you need to advance the Kingdom of God!

HELPS

It can sometimes be confusing to know where to go, in the Bible, to search for a helpful scripture. These days we have apps on our phones, and programs on our computers, but without the right context, or reference, we can come up short. I encourage you to spend some time each day studying your Bible, and becoming familiar with the wonderful text God has given us to enrich and guide our lives. I have included some scripture highlighting each of the 'Fruits of the Spirit' mentioned in Galatians chapter 5, for further reading. Be blessed and remember, you are loved by the King!

FRUITS OF THE SPIRIT

Love: John 13:1; 1 Corinthians 13:3

Joy: John 17:13; Proverbs 15:13

Peace: Philippians 4:7; Matthew 5:9

Patience: Romans 12:12; James 1:3-12

Kindness: Ephesians 4:32

Goodness: Matthew 19:16

Faithfulness: Hebrews 11:1; 1 Corinthians 12:9

Gentleness: Philippians 4:5; 2 Timothy 2:24

Self-Control: 1 Thessalonians 5:22

www.ingramcontent.com/pod-product-compliance
Lightning Source LLC
Chambersburg PA
CBHW071259110526
44591CB00010B/718